3 1994 01386 7194

SANTA ANA PUBLIC LIBRARY

D0520703

Creation of the Modern Middle East

Iraq

Creation of the Modern Middle East

Iraq

J 956.7 WAG
Wagner, Heather Lehr.
Iraq
    31994013867194   5
                                      3

Heather Lehr Wagner

Introduction by
Akbar Ahmed
School of International Service
American University

CHELSEA HOUSE
P U B L I S H E R S
A Haights Cross Communications Company
Philadelphia

Frontispiece: Street Scene, Baghdad, c. 1910-1916

CHELSEA HOUSE PUBLISHERS

EDITOR IN CHIEF Sally Cheney
DIRECTOR OF PRODUCTION Kim Shinners
CREATIVE MANAGER Takeshi Takahashi
MANUFACTURING MANAGER Diann Grasse

Staff for IRAQ

EDITOR Lee Marcott
PRODUCTION ASSISTANT Jaimie Winkler
PICTURE RESEARCHER Sarah Bloom
SERIES AND COVER DESIGNER Keith Trego
LAYOUT 21st Century Publishing and Communications, Inc.

© 2003 by Chelsea House Publishers,
a subsidiary of Haights Cross Communications.
All rights reserved. Printed and bound in the United States of America.

A Haights Cross Communications ✦ Company

http://www.chelseahouse.com

3 5 7 9 8 6 4 2

Library of Congress Cataloging-in-Publication Data

Wagner, Heather Lehr.
    Iraq / Heather Lehr Wagner.
      v. cm.—(Creation of the modern Middle East)
Includes bibliographical references and index.
Contents: In search of ancient history—A new nation is created—
Independence and its consequences—Forces of war—A country in
confusion—Politics of power—Road to war—Storms in the desert.
    ISBN 0-7910-6506-5
    1. Iraq—History—20th century. [1. Iraq—History—20th century.]
I. Title. II. Series.
DS77 .W34 2002
956.704—dc21
                                                    2002007000

Table of Contents

Index to the Photographs

Creation of the Modern Middle East

Iran

Iraq

Israel

Jordan

The Kurds

Kuwait

Oman

Palestinian Authority

Saudi Arabia

Syria

Turkey

Yemen

Introduction

Akbar Ahmed

The Middle East, it seems, is always in the news. Unfortunately, most of the news is of a troubling kind. Stories of suicide bombers, hijackers, street demonstrations, and ongoing violent conflict dominate these reports. The conflict draws in people living in lands far from the Middle East; some support one group, some support another, often on the basis of kinship or affinity and not on the merits of the case.

The Middle East is often identified with the Arabs. The region is seen as peopled by Arabs speaking Arabic and belonging to the Islamic faith. The stereotype of the Arab oil sheikh is a part of contemporary culture. But both of these images—that the Middle East is in perpetual anarchy and that it has an exclusive Arab identity—are oversimplifications of the region's complex contemporary reality.

In reality, the Middle East is an area that straddles Africa and Asia and has a combined population of over 200 million people inhabiting over twenty countries. It is a region that draws the entire world into its politics and, above all, it is the land that is the birthplace of the three great Abrahamic faiths—Judaism, Christianity, and Islam. The city of Jerusalem is the point at which these three faiths come together and also where they tragically confront one another.

It is for these reasons that knowledge of the Middle East will remain of importance and that news from it will remain ongoing and interesting.

Let us consider the stereotype of the Middle East as a land of constant anarchy. It is easy to forget that some of the greatest

9

lawgivers and people of peace were born, lived, and died here. In the Abrahamic tradition these names are a glorious roll call of human history—Abraham, Moses, Jesus, and Muhammad. In the tradition of the Middle East, where these names are especially revered, people often add the blessing "Peace be upon him" when speaking their names.

The land is clearly one that is shared by the great faiths. While it has a dominant Muslim character because of the large Muslim population, its Jewish and Christian presence must not be underestimated. Indeed, it is the dynamics of the relationships between the three faiths that allow us to enter the Middle East today and appreciate the points where these faiths come together or are in conflict.

To understand the predicament in which the people of the Middle East find themselves today, it is well to keep the facts of history before us. History is never far from the minds of the people in this region. Memories of the first great Arab dynasty, the Umayyads (661-750), based in Damascus, and the even greater one of the Abbasids (750-1258), based in Baghdad, are still kept alive in books and folklore. For the Arabs, their history, their culture, their tradition, their language, and above all their religion, provide them with a rich source of pride; but the glory of the past contrasts with the reality and powerlessness of contemporary life.

Many Arabs have blamed past rulers for their current situation beginning with the Ottomans who ruled them until World War I and then the European powers that divided their lands. When they achieved independence after World War II they discovered that the artificial boundaries created by the European powers cut across tribes and clans. Today, too, they complain that a form of Western imperialism still dominates their politics and rulers.

Again, while it is true that Arab history and Arab temperament have colored the Middle East strongly, there are other distinct peoples who have made a significant contribution to the culture of the region. Turkey is one such non-Arab nation with its own language, culture, and contribution to the region through the influence of the Ottoman Empire. Memories of that period for the Arabs are mixed, but what cannot be denied are the spectacular administrative and architectural achievements of the Ottomans. It is the longest dynasty in world history, beginning in 1300 and ending after World War I in 1922, when Kemal Ataturk wished to reject the past on the way to creating a modern Turkey.

Similarly, Iran is another non-Arab country with its own rich language and culture. Based in the minority sect of Islam, the Shia, Iran has often been in opposition to its Sunni neighbors, both Arab and Turk. Perhaps this confrontation helped to forge a unique Iranian, or Persian, cultural identity that, in turn, created the brilliant art, architecture, and poetry under the Safawids (1501-1722). The Safawid period also saw the establishment of the principle of interference or participation—depending on one's perspective—in matters of the state by the religious clerics. So while the Ayatollah Khomeini was very much a late-20th century figure, he was nonetheless reflecting the patterns of Iranian history.

Israel, too, represents an ancient, non-Arabic, cultural and religious tradition. Indeed, its very name is linked to the tribes that figure prominently in the stories of the Bible and it is through Jewish tradition that memory of the great biblical patriarchs like Abraham and Moses is kept alive. History is not a matter of years, but of millennia, in the Middle East.

Perhaps nothing has evoked as much emotional and political controversy among the Arabs as the creation of the state of Israel in 1948. With it came ideas of democracy and modern culture that seemed alien to many Arabs. Many saw the wars that followed stir further conflict and hatred; they also saw the wars as an inevitable clash between Islam and Judaism.

It is therefore important to make a comment on Islam and Judaism. The roots of prejudice against Jews can be anti-Semitic, anti-Judaic, and anti-Zionist. The prejudice may combine all three and there is often a degree of overlap. But in the case of the Arabs, the matter is more complicated because, by definition, Arabs cannot be anti-Semitic because they themselves are considered Semites. They cannot be anti-Judaic, because Islam recognizes the Jews as "people of the Book."

Introduction

What this leaves us with is the clash between the political philosophy of Zionism, which is the establishment of a Jewish nation in Palestine, and Arab thought. The antagonism of the Arabs to Israel may result in the blurring of lines. A way must be found by Arabs and Israelis to live side by side in peace. Perhaps recognition of the common Abrahamic tradition is one way forward.

The hostility to Israel partly explains the negative coverage the Arabs get in the Western media. Arab Muslims are often accused of being anarchic and barbaric due to the violence of the Middle East. Yet, their history has produced some of the greatest figures in history.

Consider the example of Sultan Salahuddin Ayyoubi, popularly called Saladin in Western literature. Saladin had vowed to take revenge for the bloody massacres that the Crusaders had indulged in when they took Jerusalem in 1099. According to a European eyewitness account the blood in the streets was so deep that it came up to the knees of the horsemen.

Yet, when Saladin took Jerusalem in 1187, he showed the essential compassion and tolerance that is at the heart of the Abrahamic faiths. He not only released the prisoners after ransom, as was the custom, but paid for those who were too poor to afford any ransom. His nobles and commanders were furious that he had not taken a bloody revenge. Saladin is still remembered in the bazaars and villages as a leader of great learning and compassion. When contemporary leaders are compared to Saladin, they are usually found wanting. One reason may be that the problems of the region are daunting.

The Middle East faces three major problems that will need solutions in the twenty-first century. These problems affect society and politics and need to be tackled by the rulers in those lands and all other people interested in creating a degree of dialogue and participation.

The first of the problems is that of democracy. Although democracy is practiced in some form in a number of the Arab countries, for the majority of ordinary people there is little sense of participation in their government. The frustration of helplessness in the face of an indifferent bureaucracy at the lower levels of administration is easily converted to violence. The indifference of the state to the pressing needs of the "street" means that other non-governmental organizations can step in. Islamic organizations offering health and education programs to people in the shantytowns and villages have therefore emerged and flourished over the last decades.

The lack of democracy also means that the ruler becomes remote and autocratic over time as he consolidates his power. It is not uncommon for many rulers in the Middle East to pass on their rule to their son. Dynastic rule, whether kingly or based in a dictatorship, excludes ordinary people from a sense of participation in their own governance. They need to feel empowered. Muslims need to feel that they are able to participate in the process of government. They must feel that they are able to elect their leaders into office and if these leaders do not deliver on their promises, that they can throw them out. Too many of the rulers are nasty and brutish. Too many Muslim leaders are kings and military dictators. Many of them ensure that their sons or relatives stay on to perpetuate their dynastic rule.

With democracy, Muslim peoples will be able to better bridge the gaps that are widening between the rich and the poor. The sight of palatial mansions with security guards carrying automatic weapons standing outside them and, alongside, hovels teeming with starkly poor children is a common one in Muslim cities. The distribution of wealth must remain a priority of any democratic government.

The second problem in the Middle East that has wide ramifications in society is that of education. Although Islam emphasizes knowledge and learning, the sad reality is that the standards of education are unsatisfactory. In addition, the climate for scholarship and intellectual activity is discouraging. Scholars are too often silenced, jailed, or chased out of the country by the administration. The sycophants and the intelligence services whose only aim is to tell the ruler what he would like to hear, fill the vacuum.

Education needs to be vigorously reformed. The *madrassah,* or religious school, which is the institution that provides primary education for millions of boys in the Middle East, needs to be brought into line with the more prestigious Westernized schools reserved for the elite of the land. By allowing two distinct streams of education to develop, Muslim nations are encouraging the growth of two separate societies: a largely illiterate and frustrated population that is susceptible to leaders with simple answers to the world's problems and a small, Westernized, often corrupt and usually uncaring group of elite. The third problem facing the Middle East is that of representation in the mass media. Although this point is hard to pin down, the images in the media are creating problems of understanding and communication in the communities living in the Middle East. Muslims, for example, will always complain that they are depicted in negative stereotypes in the non-Arab media. The result of the media onslaught that plagues Muslims is the sense of anger on the one hand and the feeling of loss of dignity on the other. Few Muslims will discuss the media rationally. Greater Muslim participation in the media and greater interaction will help to solve the problem. But it is not so simple. The Israelis also complain of the stereotypes in the Arab media that depict them negatively.

Muslims are aware that their religious culture represents a civilization rich in compassion and tolerance. They are aware that given a period of stability in which they can grapple with the problems of democracy, education, and self-image they can take their rightful place in the community of nations. However painful the current reality, they do carry an idea of an ideal human society with them. Whether a Turk, or an Iranian, or an Arab, every Muslim is aware of the message that the prophet of Islam brought to this region in the seventh century. This message still has resonance for these societies. Here are words from the last address of the prophet spoken to his people:

> All of you descend from Adam and Adam was made of earth. There is no superiority for an Arab over a non-Arab nor for a non-Arab over an Arab, neither for a white man over a black man nor a black man over a white man . . . the noblest among you is the one who is most deeply conscious of God.

This is a noble and worthy message for the twenty-first century in the Middle East. Not only Muslims, but Jews and Christians would agree with it. Perhaps its essential theme of tolerance, compassion, and equality can help to rediscover the wellsprings of tradition that can both inspire and unite.

It is for these reasons that I congratulate Chelsea House Publishers for taking the initiative in helping us to understand the Middle East through this series. The story of the Middle East is, in many profound ways, the story of human civilization.

— **Dr. Akbar S. Ahmed**
The Ibn Khaldun Chair of Islamic Studies and
Professor of International Relations,
School of International Service
American University

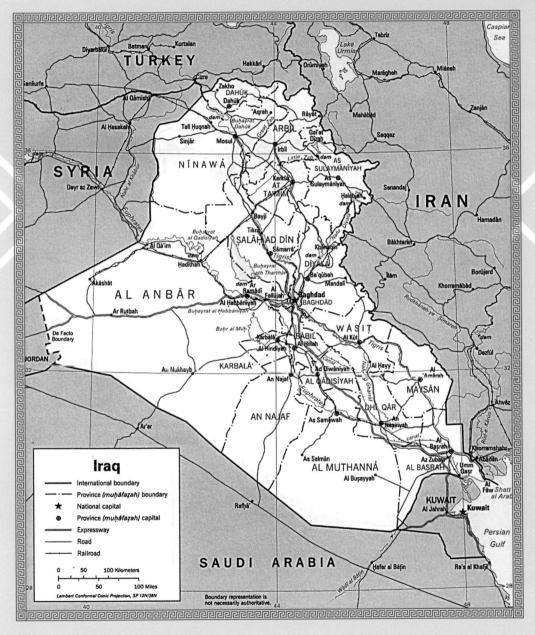

Map of modern Iraq.

Watchman's Hut, Mound at Nineveh, 1905

Nineveh was the oldest and most populous city of the ancient Assyrian Empire (858–627 B.C.). It was located on the east bank of the Tigris River opposite the modern city of Mosul.

In 1811, Claudius Rich, the British business agent in Baghdad, became the first to map ancient Nineveh, and excavations have been undertaken intermittently since then. Between 1845 and 1851, Sir Henry Layard discovered the palace of Sennacherib (705–681 B.C.). Layard sent to England an unrivaled collection of stone bas-reliefs together with thousands of cuneiform tablets from the library of Ashurbanipal (668–627 B.C.), the last great Assyrian king. These tablets are now in the British Museum in London.

During 1931–32, R. Campbell-Thompson and Sir Max Mallowan dug a shaft from the top of Nineveh mound, 90 feet above the level of the plain, through the strata of accumulated debris of earlier cultures to virgin soil. This shaft was located near the watchman's hut in this photograph. Excavations continued at Nineveh in the 1950s and 1960s but were halted when Saddam Hussein came to power in 1979.

1

In Search of
Ancient History

t was 5 A.M. and Max Mallowan was riding his horse up the slippery, muddy path to the top of the mound at Nineveh in northern Iraq. For the young British archeologist, the day always began with the same routine: First, he made a careful study of the weather with his boss, Dr. Reginald Campbell-Thompson. It was autumn and the rainy season, and conditions were often difficult. Once they had agreed that the weather was acceptable and digging at the site could proceed, Max would signal with a light to the night watchman. The watchman would then light his lamp at the top of the mound, a sign to the workers (who had to travel several miles to reach the site) that they should come to work that day.

For Max, the opportunity to search for buried treasure at Nineveh was an exciting one. Researchers had been hunting for historical records from the ancient land of the Sumerians in southern Iraq and for evidence of the civilization of the Assyrians in northern Iraq, but in that year, 1931, archeologists were beginning to search for examples of life that dated back to prehistoric times, before written records existed. The site at Nineveh was rich with hints of a civilization that flourished before recorded time.

The contents of the enormous mound at Nineveh, Max's research indicated, were three-quarters prehistoric. As the workers dug deeper and deeper, they uncovered evidence of civilizations that existed before the ancient Assyrians, though the precise dating of the bits of pottery they found was not easy.

The beauty of this part of northern Iraq was all around them—the snow-covered Kurdish mountains, the Tigris River, and, in the distance, the gleaming minarets of the city of Mosul. Max had been joined at the site by his wife, the mystery writer Agatha Christie, who had traveled from England to spend the months before Christmas by his side. One day, taking a break from the hard work, they rented a car and set off to find the site of another, much earlier, archeological dig—at Nimrud, which had last been explored by archeologists nearly a hundred years earlier. The rains made the roads difficult to travel, but eventually he and Agatha found the spot. It was a beautiful place a mile from the Tigris; as they picnicked at the peaceful site, giant stone Assyrian heads rising up from the ground, the remains of those earlier excavations, kept watch.

Max laid out a plan for his wife: someday they would return to this place, only he would be leading his own archeological team rather than working as someone's assistant. They would continue the work at Nimrud that had begun a hundred years earlier and they would, he was certain, discover great things.

THE TREASURES OF NIMRUD

It would be some 20 years before Max's dream would come true, but the discoveries he made at Nimrud in the 1950s were extraordinary. The ancient civilizations that had flourished in Iraq were among the world's earliest. The land had once been known as *Mesopotamia*, or "Land Between the Rivers," for its position between the Tigris and Euphrates rivers. It had been the home of the ancient Assyrians, the Sumerians—the land of the famed city of Babylon—and from this once-fertile territory had now come some of the world's greatest evidence of early life. Nineveh, where Max had assisted Dr. Campbell-Thompson in the 1930s, had been the political capital of Assyria while Nimrud had been the military capital, and Max was confident that this site still had many important secrets to reveal.

Indeed, Max's instinct proved correct. Early on, the site produced valuable objects made of ivory, engraved shells containing cosmetics, and fragments of cuneiform writing on wax. Max's team uncovered monuments indicating that the city had been completed in 879 B.C., as well as records telling of a banquet served over 10 days to 7,000 people to celebrate the occasion of the city's completion.

Many years later, Agatha would recall the excitement of one day, when workers who were exploring a series of brick-lined wells rushed in shouting, "We have found a woman in the well! There is a woman in the well!" They brought in a giant mound of mud and, after gentle cleaning, an ivory head emerged bearing a smiling face with black hair that had been carefully preserved in the mud for 2,500 years. The team also found an ivory carving showing a man being attacked by a lioness amid a cluster of papyrus reeds and lotus flowers; the flowers were decorated with jewels and the man's hair gleamed with

Taq Kisra, Ctesiphon, 1901

The ancient city of Ctesiphon is located on the northeast bank of the Tigris River about 20 miles southeast of Baghdad. It was the capital of the Parthian Empire (c. 320 B.C.–224 A.D.) and later of the Sassanians (224 –651 A.D.). The site is famous for the remains of a gigantic vaulted hall, the Taq Kisra, which traditionally has been considered the palace of the Sassanian King Khosrow I (531–579 A.D.). The hall has one of the largest single-span brick arches in the world.

In 637 A.D., the Arabs conquered the city and used the Taq Kisra as a mosque. But within 100 years, the new city of Baghdad had superseded Ctesiphon. Its deserted ruins were used as a quarry for building material. This photograph was presented to the Royal Geographic Society in 1901 by Sir J. B. Goldsmid.

real gold. Max discovered a tablet listing the military supplies at Nimrud, including a collection of 36,242 bows, most likely used by an army twice as large.

At the edge of Nimrud, the team uncovered traces of a mighty palace with 200 rooms covering nearly 12 acres. The palace had been the home of King Shalmaneser, and in one room they found the base of his throne, decorated with pictures of the highlights of his reign. The palace revealed spectacular murals, ivory carvings, sections of the rooms once belonging to the queen, and even rooms that had housed a harem.

OTHER EXPLORERS, OTHER TREASURES

Over 10 years, Max and his team uncovered the wonders of an ancient city piece by piece, revealing glimpses of Iraq's history that before had only been guessed at. And Max's team was not the only one digging through dirt and sand to find the glories of lost worlds. Max had begun his career working for the famous British archeologist Leonard Wooley, who had led a dig at the site of the ancient Sumerian city of Ur, in southern Iraq, from 1921 to 1934. Wooley believed that, in the pale sands of the desert there, he had found the home of Abraham, who, according to the Bible, was the father of the Hebrew people. Whether the house Wooley's team uncovered belonged to the biblical Abraham or not is still being debated by archeological researchers, but the team made many other amazing finds, including the remains of the petite Queen Puabi in a tomb filled with gold, jewels, statues, and musical instruments. The queen, who died at Ur nearly 600 years before Abraham was born, was buried with a large gold headpiece that measured nearly a foot high, and her tomb also held the remains of 21 servants who were killed or killed themselves in order to be with her in death.

Wooley's discoveries at Ur told scholars much about the history and culture of ancient Sumeria. They also provide glimpses of the Middle East we know today, including such familiar elements as streets lined with open booths, much like the bazaars still found in parts of modern Iraq. The first written evidence of the existence of medical doctors was discovered on a tablet at Ur dating back to 2700 B.C. But it is in the splendor of the tombs and palaces that the vastness of this once-mighty civilization was most clearly revealed.

The promise of ancient wealth and rich treasures lured many invading armies to conquer this territory throughout history and brought many archeological explorers to the area in the early part of the 20th century. It was believed by some that the Garden of Eden could be found here. In the ancient cuneiform inscriptions could be found some of the earliest examples of written language. The legends of the Tower of Babel, the Hanging Gardens of Babylon, and the empire of King Nebuchadnezzar captured the imagination of these scientific explorers, and the cuneiform writings and records they uncovered told of the ancient Assyrians and Sumerians and the wondrous civilization they built that flourished in the Middle East for some 2,000 years before slipping into the sand. The British, the French, the Germans, and the Americans all sent teams into what is now Iraq, and the treasures they discovered fill museums around the world today.

But while these discoveries showed the glories of the civilizations that had peopled the land in ancient times, the country that we know today as Iraq began taking shape only in the years following World War I. The land once known as the center of world civilization and culture, where so much of recorded ancient history took place, is now recognized mainly for its military aggression and oil production.

The Bazaar, Mosul, 1905

A bazaar is a Middle Eastern market consisting of rows of shops selling all sorts of items. An ancient tablet found near this bazaar in Mosul guaranteed that an emerald set in a gold ring would not fall out for twenty years: "If it should fall out, Elil-akh-iddin and Belshtinu shall pay to Ellileshum-iddin an indemnity of 10-mina of silver."
Mosul lies on the right bank of the Tigris River across from the ruins of the ancient Assyrian city of Nineveh, 225 miles northwest of Baghdad.

The Ottoman Turks ruled Mosul from 1534 to 1918. It was a major trading center of the Empire and the headquarters of a political subdivision (*wilayah*)—now known as Mosul Province. After World War I, Great Britain occupied Mosul until a border settlement (1926) placed the city in Iraq rather than Turkey. The status of Mosul Province was complicated by two factors—the British desire to gain oil concessions and the existence of a majority Kurdish population seeking independence from either Iraq or Turkey. Vast oil revenues would accrue from Mosul but the inclusion of well-armed and restless Kurds in the Iraqi territory would continue to plague subsequent Iraqi governments.

These photographs of Mosul were taken by R. Campbell-Thompson, a noted archaeologist and an expert on the Hittites, an ancient people who lived in east central Anatolia. Between 1929 and 1932, Thompson excavated the Temple of Nabu (Nebo), a major god in the Assyrian-Babylonian pantheon, at Nineveh.

Ruins of Ancient Babylon, C. 1920

Babylon had been a major urban center from the second millennium B.C. through the third century A.D. Under the Persians (539–331 B.C.), Babylon was considered the world's most splendid city. However, the present site, about 55 miles south of Baghdad, is an extensive field of ruins.

What happened to this place, located at the eastern edge of the Arab world, to shape its modern history? How did a land that produced the earliest forms of writing and the first code of laws became feared for its ability to produce weapons of mass destruction?

While Leonard Wooley, Max Mallowan, and others were digging through the earth for evidence of the ancient history of Iraq, a brand-new nation was taking shape around them.

Carving from the Ishtar Gate, Babylon

Ancient Mesopotamia's contributions to civilization were many and varied. The development of writing, based on drawings which evolved into a script known as cuneiform, the use of the wheel, metal working, and monumental temples all were established by the third millennium B.C. The Sumerians and their successors also wrote poetry, including the world's first epic, the story of Gilgamesh. This poem contains the first written account of the great flood; a later version appeared in the Old Testament.

The Ishtar Gate was an enormous brick entryway over the main thoroughfare of ancient Babylon. It was decorated with brick reliefs of dragons and young bulls, such as the one In the photograph. From the gate ran a stone paved avenue, the so-called Processional Way, which has been traced for more than half a mile.

The Lion, Babylon

This larger-than-life-size lion, probably of Hittite origin and brought to Babylon in antiquity, stands north of the Ishtar Gate.

Safinah, 1912

The safinah is a traditional sailing craft still in use along the Tigris and Euphrates rivers. The boat is 30 to 80 feet long, with a capacity of up to 50 tons.

From the dawn of civilization, the Tigris and Euphrates rivers have provided the irrigation that makes life possible for those inhabiting the flat, dry plains through which they flow. The two rivers united the populations of the north and south and gave them a common interest in controlling them and their tributaries. The rivers also were the principal arteries for trade and communication, without which the cities for which Mesopotamia is famous could not have flourished. Whatever else may divide them, the people who live along the riverbanks are conscious of their dependence on these two great rivers.

2

A New Nation Is Created

any of the countries of the Middle East that we know today—such as Saudi Arabia, Israel, or Iraq—could not be found on a map before World War I. The land was there, of course, and the people as well, but the names with which we identify specific people and places in that part of the world today were not used more than a hundred years ago. If you look at a map of the region drawn at the very beginning of the 20th century, you will find unfamiliar names and unusual boundaries defining countries much larger than those on a modern map.

In the ancient Middle East, conquering armies charged in and snatched up immense expanses of land, building empires that lasted for centuries before being swept away by the next set of conquerors.

Maps from the early 1900s reveal this history. The region was divided into huge sections, marked by names like Turkestan, Persia, and Mesopotamia, that stretched from the Mediterranean Sea to the Indian subcontinent in vast, empty expanses with few additional markings for cities or smaller territories.

For a thousand years, the land now known as Iraq had been conquered by a series of fierce warriors on horseback, who came from central and northeast Asia and seized the terrain over which they traveled as they headed west. The Ottomans took the territories of modern Iraq in about 1500 A.D. Turkish speakers and followers of the Islamic faith, these conquerors at one time held within their empire most of the Middle East, northern Africa, and parts of Europe. At the beginning of the 20th century, the region we now know as Iraq was still considered to be part of the Ottoman Empire.

The empire's economic growth depended on slave labor and on its ability to continue to invade new lands, seize the goods, and capture new slaves, as well as to expand the market for trade in Ottoman goods. But it became increasingly difficult for the empire's leaders to govern so many different peoples, keep so many territories in line, and ensure that orders were followed while also continuing to conquer new regions. The Ottomans were quite good at conquering, but not so good at governing.

While the territories of the Ottoman Empire spoke many different languages and represented many diverse ethnic backgrounds, the single element that drew all the regions together was religion. The Ottoman Empire was a Muslim state, yet even within that simple framework, differences emerged. Two groups, or *sects*, existed: the *Sunnis*, representing the largest number of Muslims within the empire and who regarded the Ottoman leaders as spiritual guides and the successors to the prophet Muhammad; and the *Shi'ites*, who disagreed with many of the Ottoman policies and did

Funeral Wagons, 1909

These funeral wagons, usually drawn by four mules, were used to travel between Baghdad and Karbala', a distance of 55 miles.

Karbala' is Iraq's foremost holy city. Husayn, the grandson of Muhammad, was killed at the Battle of Karbala', between the Sunni and Shi'ite sects of Islam, in 680 A.D. Shi'ites observe the day of Husayn's death, the 10th of Muharram in the Islamic calendar, as a day of public mourning. Revenge for Husayn's death contributed to a major split in Islam and gave impetus to the rise of the powerful Shi'ite movement. His tomb remains one of the greatest Shi'ite shrines and pilgrimage centers. Shi'ite Muslims consider burial in Karbala' a sure means of reaching paradise; therefore, the city has a large number of cemeteries.

not support their claim to be the rightful spiritual and religious leaders of the people they ruled.

So, as the winds of war slowly swept over the globe at the beginning of the 20th century, drawing nation after nation into the conflict that became World War I, the empire the Ottomans had built in the Middle East was crumbling. Young, ambitious political leaders in Turkey seized power and attempted to launch reforms to hold the territory together. But it was too little, too late. Other powers and other nations had moved into the region, recognizing the opportunities the weakened Ottoman Empire presented and sensing the wealth that lay beneath the desert sand. Just a short time earlier, the great powers of Europe had carved up Africa. Now they turned their eyes to the Middle East. The British, the French, the Germans, and the Russians all were viewed with trepidation by the remnants of the Ottoman leadership.

A REMARKABLE WOMAN

When you think of the powerful leaders whose words and actions shaped the modern history of Iraq, you may picture nomadic tribesmen in traditional desert robes, or prime ministers and statesmen from the various parts of Europe, building railroads and trade routes leading them deep into the territories of the Middle East. You may imagine the military men whose campaigns brought them fame and resulted in expansion of the lands controlled by their nations. But it was a woman named Gertrude Bell who actually shaped the destiny of the land that today we call Iraq.

A courageous and accomplished British traveler, Bell was described by some as the "Desert Queen." Through her letters and books, she painted a picture of the Mesopotamian region that showed, in truer colors than ever before, the vastness and richness of the land and its people. Her words influenced the British statesmen who became her friends, and her thoughts and ideas greatly contributed to establishment of the borders and government that shape Iraq even to this day.

Gertrude Bell was born on July 14, 1868, in Durham, England, to a wealthy family. Her mother died when she was only three years old. Her father, a highly educated and successful man, encouraged his daughter's curiosity and sent her away to school in London when she was 15. This was an unusual step in the late 1800s, when most of the girls of Gertrude's social class and background were educated at

Bedouin, 1906

The Bedouins are an Arab people who are nomadic herders in the deserts of the Middle East.

Bedouins who follow their traditional way of life travel the deserts seeking water and pasture for their camels, goats, and sheep. They live in tents and wear clothing made from the skin and hair of their animals. The Bedouins eat mostly dairy products, dates, and rice. They trade meat from their livestock for knives, pots, and other manufactured goods of the people in nearby villages.

Since the 1950s, an increasing number of Bedouins have abandoned their nomadic life. Many have taken advantage of programs that encourage them to settle on land where they can farm. It is estimated that the total number of Bedouins today is about one million.

This photograph was taken in Assur, modern Qal' at Sharqat, the ancient religious capital of Assyria, located on the west bank of the Tigris River in northern Iraq.

home by tutors and then, when they reached the age of 17, were presented to society. The goal for girls of that time was to find a good husband, and they were expected to marry before they turned 20.

But Gertrude's father was a more progressive thinker. He recognized Gertrude's intelligence and encouraged her to use her mind. She was an excellent student and, at 18, she decided to attend Oxford University. In 1886, when Bell first entered Oxford, the presence of women in the classroom was rare. In fact, in the university's 700-year history to that point, women had been allowed to attend for only the seven years prior to Bell's arrival there. And although they were allowed to attend the lectures, the handful of young women students were expected to sit separately from the young men, sometimes on the same raised platform from which the professor lectured, placing them directly in front of the curious and unfriendly eyes of the male students. One history professor allowed Bell in his class only if she sat in the room with her back to him! Despite these obstacles, Bell performed brilliantly and earned the highest mark (called a First) in Modern History. She was the first woman to do so, an accomplishment so newsworthy that it was published in the London *Times*.

But for young women of that Victorian era, educational accomplishments meant little—the most important goal was to marry. By the time she was 23, Bell was still unmarried and feeling quite lonely. When her aunt invited her to join her on a trip to Persia (a region that we know today as Iran), Bell spent several months studying the language and familiarizing herself with the customs of the people. In the spring of 1892, she set out from the cold gray of England, boarded the Orient Express from Paris to Constantinople, and then traveled by boat to Persia. The young woman who set out from Europe that spring and emerged into the dazzling colors of the Middle East was soon to become a transformed person. In a letter to her cousin written two months after her

Basra, 1891

The principal Christian and Jewish merchants of Basra.

Because of Basra's strategic location at the head of the Persian Gulf, this ancient city, founded in the seventh century A.D., changed hands numerous times. Nevertheless, Basra became a brilliant cultural center in its own right. It was home to noted Arab grammarians, poets, and religious scholars. Basra is perhaps best known to Westerners as the city from which Sinbad the Sailor set sail in *The Thousand and One Nights.*

arrival, she said, "Are we the same people, I wonder, when all our surroundings, associations, acquaintances are changed?" The Middle East would shape Gertrude Bell's destiny, just as clearly as she shaped its own.

ARABIAN ADVENTURES

That first trip to Persia sparked a new life for Bell. Although she returned from time to time to visit family in England, she found an excitement in the Middle East that made life at home seem dull and drab. She enjoyed great freedom in the new lands she explored; the rules and customs that governed a woman's behavior in strict Victorian England had little meaning in the desert.

Her study habits served her well. Unlike many travelers to foreign countries, she made a point of learning the customs and the languages of the places she visited. She learned to carry on a conversation in French, Italian, German, Persian, Turkish, and Arabic, and this skill (acquired only after years of study) made it possible for her to live comfortably among the people she encountered on her travels. She quickly moved beyond the places well traveled by tourists and often headed out on horseback, accompanied by a few native guides, to the desert. There, she encountered tribesmen and nomads who, suspicious of the British woman at first, grew to accept and even trust her as they shared confidences in their native language over cups of strong Turkish coffee.

Bell learned much about the local politics as she traveled through the crumbling Ottoman territories. She returned to England to write a book that contained descriptions and photographs of what she had seen in the Middle East. It was immediately successful, and it marked her as an expert in the culture of the Middle East. Other books and articles would follow.

Bell decided to acquire a new set of skills while she was in England. She learned surveying, how to chart position and direction based on the stars, and some basic techniques for mapmaking. She returned to the Middle East, this time with a new goal: she would visit Mesopotamia and create maps of the uncharted deserts there.

Her travels took her into unfamiliar and often danger-ous regions. War had broken out among some of the desert tribes, and she was captured and held prisoner for 10 days by one wealthy tribal leader. Water and food supplies frequently ran low. And yet Bell journeyed on, photograph-ing and taking notes for the books and articles that would

Camel Caravan, 1912

The combination of rain shortage and extreme heat makes much of Iraq a desert. In these areas, the inhabitants still rely on camels for transportation.

Because of very high rates of evaporation, soil and plants rapidly lose the little moisture obtained from rain. Vegetation cannot survive without extensive irrigation.

The Iraqi desert, which is west and southwest of the Euphrates River, is part of the great Syrian Desert, which covers sections of Syria, Jordan, and Saudi Arabia. Pastoral nomads inhabit this vast area. They rely on *wadis*—water channels that are dry most of the year. Some wadis are more than 200 miles long and carry brief but torrential flood waters during the winter rains.

open up the mysteries of Mesopotamia to British readers.

Among those who followed her adventures with great interest were British politicians, who recognized the opportunities the collapsing Ottoman Empire held. By 1908, Constantinople, the capital of the Ottoman Empire, was in chaos. A group of students from the universities and military academies there, who became known as "the Young Turks," had forced the sultan to resign and taken over the government. But the new government they formed faced financial problems and they were eager to borrow money and aid from the Europeans, who were happy to oblige in return for firming up their position in the region.

Germany was particularly interested in the area and had a good relationship with the Young Turks, since the majority of the military academies many of them had attended were run by German officers. At the beginning of the 20th century, Germany was also constructing a strategic railroad line to run from Berlin to Baghdad. This railroad threatened the security of the British, who worried about the increasing German presence in a region that was important in part because it lay along the route to India, the "crown jewel" in the British Empire of the time.

In addition, by 1911 the British navy was switching its mighty battleships from coal-burning engines to oil, making it possible for them to travel farther and faster and be refueled at sea. While Britain had plenty of coal, it had no oil, and was eager to find a steady supply in the Middle East.

Thus, Bell's knowledge of the region and her familiarity with the local politics and important players made her a great resource to British leaders. Ambassadors and foreign secretaries relied on her information, and as the conflict that broke out in Sarajevo (Yugoslavia) in 1914 quickly engulfed Europe, Britain's need for precious Middle Eastern oil became even more urgent. In late 1915, Bell was asked by British military intelligence to go to Cairo, Egypt, to help

British and Indian Troops Entering Baghdad, 1917

British rule (1917–32) shaped modern Iraq. Before the British mandate, there was no Iraq; after it, a new state with a modern government came into being. Along with the creation of the country, Great Britain bequeathed Iraq its present boundaries, and the ensuing Kurdish and border problems with its neighbors.

At the outbreak of World War I in 1914, Great Britain had no intention of occupying the Tigris and Euphrates valley. However, when it became apparent late in 1914 that Turkey, Britain's traditional ally, would enter the war on the side of the Central Powers, the British sent forces into Basra, located at the head of the Persian Gulf. The goal was to protect Britain's oil interests.

By the end of 1916, Great Britain's position changed again. Secret agreements had been concluded with the Sharif Hussein, the emir of Mecca, and with the French. These agreements recognized Britain's right to formally administer the Basra and Baghdad *wilayahs*. (Under the Ottomans, Iraq had been divided into three *wilayahs*, or provinces—Basra, Baghdad, and Mosul.) In March 1917, the British took Baghdad, and in 1918, just prior to the surrender of the Ottomans, the British moved into Mosul and its many oil fields. The occupation of Mosul was to become a cause of contention between the British and the Turks, with the latter claiming that it was not included under the terms of the surrender armistice.

By November 1918, the British wartime conquest of most of Iraq was complete.

with the war effort by providing valuable insight into the impact the war was having on the Middle East.

After a few months in Egypt, Bell was sent on to the region of Mesopotamia to collect information from the Arabs and to share what she learned with the British intelligence service.

FROM SPY TO KINGMAKER

The information Bell gathered was equally useful after World War I ended. Britain occupied Mesopotamia, but British politicians held deeply divided opinions about how best to handle this new territory. Sir Arnold Wilson, the British officer responsible for managing the region from 1918 to 1920, felt that the territory should become a British protectorate, linked to India and governed by Indian immigrants who had bravely served the British Empire during the war. But Bell, who was by then working for Sir Arnold, felt differently, and she and others in the region argued equally strongly that the region should be governed by Arabs.

It quickly became clear that while British popular opinion supported many different options, there was one point of agreement: the former Ottoman provinces in the region needed a new system of government.

Local trouble began not long after World War I ended, when the League of Nations began carving up the former Ottoman Empire, officially giving different portions to the victorious Allied forces. At the San Remo Conference of April 25, 1920, Prime Minister Lloyd George of Britain and Premier Georges Clemenceau of France reached an agreement on how to divide the Arab region: Arabia would remain independent; Syria (including Lebanon) would be mandated to the French; and Mesopotamia and Palestine would be mandated to the British. While the French agreed to grant Mosul in northern Mesopotamia to the British, it was only with the understanding that both France and Britain would share in oil exploration and production there.

With this meeting, the fate of the Middle East was seemingly decided without Arabic participation or consultation. When the news reached the people of Mesopotamia, they were outraged. In June 1920, a sheikh who had been imprisoned by the British for refusing to pay a debt launched a revolt that spread throughout the tribal areas near the Euphrates and on to the regions north and east of Baghdad, destroying railroad tracks and bridges in the process. The British brought in the Royal Air Force to bomb the troubled areas. By the time the revolt ended, 400 British had been killed and £40 million had been spent to bring the region back under control. To the British public back in England, it was a ridiculous waste of lives and money. The outcry was clear: it was time to pull back from the region, and British politicians began to look for a leader with an Arab background but who would still be friendly to British interests.

In October 1920, Sir Percy Cox returned to the region as the British government's high commissioner. Sir Percy had lived for many years in Arab countries, and was respected for his sensitivity to Arab sentiments as well as for his political skills. It was during the celebration to herald Sir Percy's return that the name "Iraq" was first used officially by the British. On that date of October 11, 1920, Sir Percy promised that Iraq would belong to and be ruled by the Arabic people. He then immediately set to work to make his promise a reality while ensuring that Britain would retain the strategic and economic position it required in the region.

Gertrude Bell supported Sir Percy's position of Arabic rule. Her contacts among a wide range of Iraqi people made her invaluable as the search began for an appropriate leader. Gertrude met with tribesmen and townsmen, military and religious leaders, all in an effort to find out who might most easily win public support and avoid another disastrous revolt.

In the end, it was a foreigner who was chosen as the future king of Iraq. Faysal, the son of the Sharif Hussein of Mecca, had recently lost his throne in Syria after being sent into exile by the French. A quiet, serious man, Faysal had been the middle son in a powerful political family, and his rise to the throne of Iraq would spark great envy in his brothers. He was a controversial choice—the language he spoke was different from the Arabic of the Iraqi people he would need to govern; he was from Mecca (Arabia), not Iraq; and he clearly had strong ties to the British. Nevertheless, the British were committed to pulling back from their involvement in the region and needed a local leader to quiet the complaints of both the natives in Iraq, who resented the British presence in their homeland, and the people back in England, who resented the cost of the Middle East efforts.

So it was that in March 1921 a group of representatives gathered in Cairo to decide the future of Iraq. Winston Churchill, at the time an official with the British Colonial Office, described the group as "Forty Thieves," although they really numbered 38. They were considered to be the leading experts on the Middle East, and Gertrude Bell was among them. During this conference, representatives sketched out the boundaries of what would become the kingdom of Iraq. They agreed on the appointment of Faysal as king, and discussed the best ways to ensure that he would be accepted by the Iraqi people.

It was agreed that Faysal's suitability as king depended on his acceptability to the people on both religious as well as political grounds. As a member of the royal Sharifian family, Faysal was considered to be a descendent of the prophet Muhammad, the central religious figure in Islam. To emphasize this connection, the Cairo Conference agreed that Faysal would need to go to Mecca, the birthplace of Muhammad and considered the holiest of all places in Islam. From there, he would travel to Iraq, as if he had been summoned by the Iraqi people to lead them on a pilgrimage to power, providing them with both a spiritual and political leadership that had been lacking under the British.

The challenges that faced Faysal were overwhelming. He was a Sunni Muslim, ruling a country in which the majority of the people were Shi'ite. The provinces that had been divided by the Ottomans into different territories (Baghdad, Basra, and Mosul) and that were now to be united as part of his kingdom varied greatly in their religious and ethnic communities. In the north lay Kurdistan, a region whose people spoke a different language altogether (Kurdish) and considered themselves to be more closely connected to other Kurdish people in Turkey than to the Iraqi people who were now their countrymen. Also, the cities of the new kingdom contained large populations of Christians and Jews. For Faysal, the task was enormous: he would be a new king in a new nation, trying to gather up the strands of an empire the British found too expensive to govern.

At the time of his coronation, on August 23, 1921, Faysal was 36 years old. A new flag was raised over the new nation, and a proclamation declared that 96 percent of the people of Mesopotamia had elected him king. The British were relieved at this solution to their problems. They felt confident that they could continue to influence the direction of the country while allowing it to be governed by Arabs.

Gertrude Bell was among the most enthusiastic supporters of Faysal. She made a great effort to educate him

King Faysal I of Iraq

In March 1921 a group of representatives gathered in Cairo to decide the future of Iraq. They agreed on the appointment of Faysal as king. But although Faysal was considered to be a descendent of the prophet Muhammed, he would be a Sunni Muslim ruling in a country that was largely Shi'ite, and faced other obstacles as well.

in the wonders of his new kingdom, inviting archeologists (among them Leonard Wooley) to lecture on the treasures of the digs and providing his staff with instructions about the ceremonies that should play a part in the life of the court. Neither she nor her British countrymen fully understood that Faysal and the Iraqi people had no intention of being guided through the process of governing their own country. They wished to shape their own destiny, and the route they intended to take required complete independence.

Although it was not clear in the beginning, the British influence on Iraq was waning. Gertrude Bell was an early casualty. Having been involved so closely in the early days, shaping Iraq's destiny from the largest scale (helping to decide where the boundaries of the new country would be drawn) to the smaller details (deciding on an appropriate design for the new nation's flag), Bell found her role greatly diminished in the new monarchy. She became involved in establishing a museum to safeguard the antiquities emerging from Iraq's archeological sites, but the excitement and intrigue she had enjoyed as a source of critical information for the British and Arabs alike was gone. She was ill-suited to a quiet life of garden parties and picnics and became depressed by the downturn in her own usefulness and by her family's economic struggles after the war. On July 11, 1926, she took her own life. The kingdom that she had helped to build would outlast her by only 12 years.

Mosul, 1905

The British consular agent at Mosul and his family. It was customary for Britain to employ local prominent persons to represent their commercial interests.

3

Independence and Its Consequences

Before becoming king, Faysal was a respected military leader. He had led an Arab army in battles against the Ottomans, and his ability to unite many different forces under a single banner of Arab unity served him well in his early days of ruling Iraq. The people were deeply divided into three groups: those who felt a loyalty to the British and wished to continue the mandate granting Britain 20 years to oversee Iraq; those who wished for independence and full Arab control; and those who still felt greater ties to the old Ottoman Empire and wished to reestablish a connection with Turkey.

King Faysal expertly balanced these conflicting demands and moved smoothly among the differing factions, seeming to agree with each group yet at the same time steadily moving Iraq in the direction he felt was best.

But the clique with which Faysal felt most comfortable consisted of other military officers who shared many of the same experiences: Ottoman military training, similar schooling, and a Sunni perspective on religion. One of his close advisers was Nuri as-Said, a military officer who had first served in the Turkish army and then later followed Faysal's leadership into the Arab army that revolted against Ottoman rule.

Nuri as-Said was born in Baghdad in 1888, and so offered the king an adviser who was also a native of the region. He ultimately became prime minister of Iraq in 1930. In that position, he was faced with the challenge of negotiating a new treaty with the British.

RUMBLINGS OF INDEPENDENCE

The first treaty with Britain had been signed shortly after Faysal was crowned king. As a formal documentation of the relationship between Iraq and Britain, the treaty was to make clear that the terms of the mandate put into place by the League of Nations would largely be left in place by the new Iraqi government. Iraq agreed to cooperate with the League of Nations, to respect religious freedom, to allow missionaries to continue their work, to respect the rights of foreigners, and to treat all states equally. The agreement stated that Britain would be consulted on foreign and domestic matters, including military efforts, judicial decisions, and financial concerns. In return, Britain agreed to prepare Iraq for membership in the League of Nations, although the time frame for this was extremely vague. The treaty, signed on October 10, 1922, was meant to last for 20 years.

But as time passed, Faysal felt strongly that the 20-year period of British oversight was far too long. This was not the kingdom he intended to rule—a kingdom essentially operating under the scrutiny of a British microscope. And the British public was equally displeased. There had been a movement in England to drastically reduce expenses in Iraq. The people wanted an assurance that this would happen quickly, not over a 20-year period. So, less than a year later, on April 30, 1923, the treaty was changed, shortening the period of time that Britain would oversee Iraq to four years.

The next step was for Iraq to draw up its own constitution. Finally drafted, adopted, and signed by the king in March 1925, the new constitution specified that Iraq would be ruled by a monarchy, that the government would follow a parliamentary format, and that the legislature would consist of two parts—an elected House of Representatives and an appointed Senate.

The system of government chosen was similar in nature to that of Britain, and it made it possible for the British to continue to operate behind the scenes, dictating policy and influencing decision making. And despite the fact that there was an elected group of representatives, the king held the power to call for new elections whenever he wanted, and to create or dismiss cabinets and prime ministers at will. As a result, the king held a great deal of power over all the elected officials. If a member of his cabinet became too powerful, the king would dismiss him. Because there was a limited group of politicians in Iraq that had the necessary experience, the king would frequently hire and fire the same people several times over.

Nuri as-Said is one example of this revolving door; he served as prime minister 14 different times. Between 1920 and 1936, there were 21 different cabinets, and only

27 people held the top positions. In that group, there were 14 men making the key decisions while constantly moving in and out of office, changing jobs, being fired and rehired at the king's whim.

Chaos was inevitable. Rumblings had begun among the Iraqi people that full independence was the only way for Iraq to take its rightful place in the Arab world. Revolts continued on small scales throughout the country. As the British army began to pull out of the farthest stretches of the country, those responsible for the revolts became bolder in their cries against the British. Different parts of the country were pulling away from the center.

Faysal and others in his government felt that Iraq could never fully develop, either politically or economi- cally, while it was still necessary to check any and all major decisions with Britain. He and other political officers who had been trained in German military schools in the old days of the Ottoman Empire had been greatly impressed by the German emphasis on national- ism—on pride in one's country. The German history contained similar experiences of uniting diverse groups under a single banner of national pride, and Faysal took those lessons seriously. It seemed clear that Iraq must be able to govern itself without a foreign power overseeing its efforts.

In response to the demands of the British and Iraqi people, Britain eventually agreed to end what had become an unworkable system. Nuri as-Said, serving then in one of his many stints as prime minister, worked hard to develop a more sensible agreement with Britain and, in 1929, Britain agreed to sponsor Iraq for admission into the League of Nations as a first step toward independence. But the new agreement still left a significant portion of foreign policy decision making in British hands. And while the British agreed to provide aid, equipment, and training to the Iraqi armed forces, they were also allowed to use all Iraqi railroads, airports, and seaports in the event of war. In addition, both Iraq and Britain agreed to take the same defensive position in the event of war—in other words, if war was declared, they would fight on the same side. The treaty was ratified in June 1930, at a time when Iraq's focus was much more on national than international worries. The prospect of war seemed far away.

A POWER STRUGGLE

On October 3, 1932, Iraq was admitted to the League of Nations as an independent state. Nuri as-Said had played an important role in leading Iraq into the League—too important, perhaps—at least in the king's eyes. Always suspicious of anyone whose power might challenge his own, King Faysal decided that as-Said must go. Upon his return from Geneva and the triumph of seeing Iraq admitted into the League of Nations, as-Said received a telegram from the king. The message: he had been fired.

Having begun the process of removing British influence from his government (by both removing Nuri as-Said and achieving independence for his country), King Faysal turned his attention to unifying all the different political groups. Those who had once passionately argued against Faysal's government, claiming that he was too dependent on the British, could now be drawn in. The king invited Rashi Ali al-Gaylari, a leader of one of the opposition movements that had struggled against him, to become prime minister in the new government. And, true to the nature of Iraqi politics, Nuri as-Said was soon back too, this time as foreign minister.

Desert Police, c. 1935

When the British mandate ended in 1932, Iraq's political leaders almost continually argued, causing bitter internal dissension. Questions dealing with the rights of minorities, the use of oil revenues, and, above all, power led to violence, manipulated elections, coups, and military intervention.

By 1932, the Iraqi national police had grown into a well-trained force of 8,000 as the reach of the central government was extended, slowly but surely, into the countryside. The desert police photographed here enforced tax collecting and suppressed tribal uprisings in areas where chiefs remained unfriendly to the group in power.

Not everyone was pleased at the exit of the British from Iraqi politics. The Assyrians, a small Christian community living in the north of Iraq, in Mosul, had been brought into Iraq during World War I to help fight with British troops, and after the war had received guarantees of protection from the British. Thus, as the British began to leave the country, the Assyrians became increasingly nervous. They asked for a firm pledge of protection from the new government, and, to create a greater level of security, Assyrians living in Syria moved back across the Iraqi border to Mosul, forming an even larger Assyrian community in the region.

The Assyrians were known to be anti-Arab and pro-British. What's more, they had served principally in the military, and rumors swirled among the Iraqis that they still were heavily armed. During British occupation, the Assyrians had been paid a higher wage than Iraqi troops. And even after independence, the Assyrians (under British protection) had not become Iraqi citizens, but instead maintained their small territory of independent people who were still much more loyal to Britain than to Iraq.

Trouble was clearly brewing in the north during that summer of 1933, but King Faysal picked this unfortunate time to leave his country and go to Europe. In his absence, the new government and the newly created army decided to show their strength and prove to the Iraqi people that the days of British influence were over. Troops were sent to the northern region and several hundred Assyrians were brutally killed.

The League of Nations quickly responded to this massacre—less than a year after Iraq had signed a pledge to respect the rights of minority groups living within its borders. King Faysal rushed back to Baghdad, but it was too late. Great support had developed for the army's actions, and for conscription—a draft—requiring young men to serve a fixed term in the army unless they were the chief wage earners for their families. Within three years, the size of the army doubled.

Troops returned from the Assyrian campaign in the north to victory parades. The majority of the Iraqi people were pleased with the way the army and its military officers had dealt with trouble and, at the same time, wiped out a bit more of the last traces of British power in the region. As the troops marched back home they were greeted by enthusiastic cheers for them and for their leader. But the leader receiving the applause was not Faysal; it was his son, Ghazi. When Faysal realized he could not control the situation within his own country, and suffering from heart trouble, he left for Switzerland, where he died in September 1933.

WEAK KING IN A VIOLENT TIME

Ghazi was only 21 years old when he became king. His youth and inexperience placed him at a real disadvantage when faced with the crafty maneuverings of the politicians operating in Iraq. Having moved in and out of power so frequently during King Faysal's reign, people like Nuri as-Said and others were used to forming and breaking alliances, depending on what served them best, and they quickly moved in to whisper advice to the young king, most of which resulted in decisions that benefited only the whisperer.

Ghazi had supported the army's efforts against the Assyrians and encouraged the draft. The army became increasingly powerful, and it also began to play a political role as Ghazi used it to stamp out any disturbances in

King Ghazi of Iraq, September 1933

King Ghazi of Iraq, son of Faysal, became king at the age of 21. His youth and inexperience left a power vacuum for other, shrewder politicians to step in and take the reins of power.

his country and make sure that no other rebellions
sprang up in the far reaches of the land. Support of the
army also became an important factor in politicians'
success. Generally this required bribes and offers of
better housing or fine wines and food. If politicians
chose not to go along, it became increasingly difficult for
them to govern and win elections. Local revolts, riots,
and looting would be ignored by troops asked to restore
peace. In short, the politicians needed the army much
more than the army needed the politicians—a dangerous
situation in a country where the king was weak and the
nation was new.

Ghazi made matters worse by constantly consulting
military officers on everything, even nonmilitary decisions.
Thus the stage was set for the military to completely
overthrow the government in power. In 1936, Hikmat
Sulayman and a group of old politicians joined forces
with a band of young men who supported socialism and
democracy and who wanted reforms. This strange set of
allies then urged the army to attack Baghdad. It did, and
the cabinet was forced to resign. Hikmat Sulayman
became the new prime minister, and he chose as his chief
of staff a commander of a division of the army, thus
giving the military direct influence over policy. This fact
did not bring stability to the government, however, and
from 1936 to 1941, as different army officers supported
different politicians, government leadership changed
eight different times.

The turmoil was only beginning. In April 1939, King
Ghazi, who loved fast cars, was killed in an automobile
accident. His son, Faysal II, became the new king, faced
with a country fraught with problems and a government
in a constant state of chaos. The international picture
was no brighter—World War II was about to break out.

It all would have been a nearly impossible job for the most experienced of rulers, but the new king could hardly be described as wise. Faysal II, Iraq's new monarch, was only four years old.

Iraq Treaty, c. 1948

The signing of a twenty-year treaty between Iraq and Great Britain on January 15, 1948 was intended to be a victory for Iraqi interests, but instead riots broke out in Baghdad.

4

The Forces of War

hile the young Faysal II held the title of king, his actual duties were carried out by his uncle, Emir Abd al-Ilah, who had been appointed regent, which meant that he would hold this position until Faysal II was old enough to rule on his own. Abd al-Ilah was strongly pro-British, a dangerous position in a country veering violently away from the tradition of British involvement in the region.

SHIFTING ALLIANCES

Iraq's past and future collided with the outbreak of World War II in 1939. At this time, Nuri as-Said was back in power in one of his many turns as prime minister. In keeping with the 1930 agreement as-Said helped to negotiate with Britain, which stated that, in the event of war, Britain and Iraq would take the same defensive position, as-Said was prepared to declare war on Germany. But the powerful Iraqi army felt differently. Since some of the older officers had been trained in military schools operated by Germans during the Ottoman Empire, they sympathized with the motivation behind the Nazis' military actions and were able to overlook the racist aspects of Nazism that were most unflattering to Arabs. Ultimately, the officers allowed as-Said to break off diplomatic relations with Germany in September 1939, as the British had requested, but they refused to allow him to declare war on Germany or to send Iraqi troops to the Balkans to join in the Allied efforts there.

By the time Italy entered the war in June 1940, the Iraqi government had changed yet again. Nuri as-Said was out as prime minister, although he held the important position of minister of foreign affairs, and the new prime minister was Rashid Ali al-Gaylani. The king's uncle, Abd al-Ilah, was forced to flee the country. Impressed by German victories in Holland, Denmark, and Norway, and the defeat of France, the new leaders were even more certain that if they wanted to be on the winning side, they should not link themselves with Britain. At this same time, there was a renewed interest among many members of the Iraqi public in creating a kind of "brotherhood of nations" among all Arab countries. The nationalists in the Iraqi government felt that their ties to their fellow Arab nations should be of greater importance than any ties to countries far away in Europe. Both Syria and Palestine were under foreign control, and the Pan-Arabs, as they were called, felt that the first priority should be supporting the efforts of these neighboring countries to achieve independence rather than the military campaigns being waged by countries much further away.

The influence of the military officers, many of whom were pro-Germany, and the Pan-Arabs in positions of political power made it impossible for Rashid Ali al-Gaylani to support the British in their war effort. But some in the government went even further: they secretly approached the Germans in an effort to form a new alliance, this time on the side fighting the Allies.

The British were concerned at the unexpected developments in the Middle East. Apart from a very small military presence stationed on the ground in Iraq to guard British air bases, the majority of British troops in place in the region were air force personnel, not ground troops. They had depended on the Iraqi force of 46,000 troops plus 12,000 police and many former military men to back up the British presence. The news that these troops now might actually be moving toward the German side was particularly unwelcome at a time when Britain was desperately fighting for its life in Europe.

The British decided to send troops to Basra, a large city in southern Iraq where they had built a large, modern port during World War I. Strategically Basra was an important point from which to launch campaigns and carry supplies by sea, railway, or air.

For the Iraqis, the arrival of British troops was an alarming sight. Only recently had independence been achieved; they had no interest in reverting back to the days of British occupation. Rashid Ali immediately informed the British that they must move the troops out of Iraq and on to Palestine, and that no more troops could arrive until the first group had left the country. Britain refused and instead began sending additional troops to the military base at Habbaniya, 55 miles west of Baghdad.

Basra, 1891

Basra is the principal port of Iraq. Creeks and canals link the city with the
Persian Gulf. By the end of the 19th century, Basra had become an important
transhipment point for river traffic to Baghdad.

The growth of Iraq's petroleum industry turned Basra into a major
oil-refining center. The city was severely damaged during the Iran-Iraq War
(1980–88) and the Persian Gulf War (1991).

At the prospect of a large British military presence so close to the country's capital, military officials in the Iraqi government decided to take the drastic step of sending their own troops into the region to guard the base and prevent additional British troops from landing. Based on their secret negotiations with the Germans, the Iraqi military men felt confident that the Germans would come to their aid should the conflict turn into a war. The small numbers of British troops currently in place also made the Iraqis feel confident of victory.

The British had had enough. On May 2, 1941, they attacked without warning, firing missiles at and shelling the Iraqi troops around their base at Habbaniya. The Iraqis fought back. The former allies were now at war.

THE BRITISH BACK IN POWER

While the Iraqis initially held the manpower advantage at Habbaniya, the British were quick to send in additional troops from other parts of the Middle East. After four short weeks, British troops marched toward Baghdad. Iraqi leaders, including Nuri as-Said and Rashid Ali al-Gaylani, fled the country, many heading for Iran. The few who were left promptly surrendered.

Faysal II's uncle was restored to power. With a friendly ruler once more in place, a pro-British government was swiftly set up. The country declared war on Germany in January 1942, and the British promptly took advantage of Iraq's bases to reinforce their military presence in the Middle East.

During the war, martial law was in effect; restrictions were put in place to limit freedom of speech, inflation was high, and food shortages were frequent. After the war, the public expected these limitations to disappear. When they did not, public outcry was immediate.

In 1945, the king's uncle, still serving as regent, took a step to address some of the public's concerns. He felt that the country's parliamentary system needed to be strengthened, to give the people a sense that they were actively involved in their government. He called for the formation of political parties. It is perhaps not surprising that each political party that was formed appealed to a different group of people: the Pan-Arabs, who spoke out strongly against the British presence in the country; the moderates, who supported limited reforms; and various socialistically oriented parties that supported redistributing state-owned and privately owned land, improving working conditions for the poor, and increasing access to medical care and education.

In this mix of new ideas and calls for reform, the older politicians, who wanted to hold onto their power, land, and wealth, were ill at ease. But once the calls for reform began, it was difficult to quiet them. The government that had been formed after the war, in January 1946, lasted only a few short months, and then once more Nuri as-Said was back in power as prime minister. He tried to appeal to the various political parties and win their support, but he was unsuccessful. Another round of elections were called, and the political parties refused to participate, claiming that they would not be allowed to fairly join in the political process. By March 1947, as-Said had resigned and a new prime minister, the first Shi'ite politician to rise to that high a position, had been elected. Salih Jabr tried to hold together the many conflicting demands of his countrymen, but the biggest challenge he undertook—negotiating a new treaty with the British in the aftermath of World War II—ultimately cost him his job.

Traveling to London, Jabr met with the British to carve out the terms of a new agreement. The British had been burned once before, however, and did not wish to make the same mistakes again. They intended to ensure that they would retain control of their air bases in Iraq; Jabr insisted that these must be controlled by Iraqis. After some brief negotiation, it was agreed that Iraq would regain control of the air bases—Britain could only use them if Iraq agreed. In addition, the British forces would leave the country, and the Iraqi army would be given both training and weapons.

Confident that he had finalized an agreement that would win great support from his people, Jabr signed the 20-year treaty in January 1948. But he had not correctly understood how strong the anti-British sentiment had grown in his country. As news of the treaty's terms reached Iraq, riots broke out in Baghdad.

With Jabr still in London, the king's uncle called in both older and younger politicians to try to work out some sort of a reasonable solution, but with no success. The final decision by the Iraqi leadership: the treaty must go. Jabr rushed back to Baghdad to try to explain his position, but the riots continued. Jabr and his government were forced out of office, and the treaty was abandoned. The door to political power swung open once more, and once more Nuri as-Said walked in. Under his leadership, a new government was formed, filled once again with the same group of older politicians who had repeatedly held office since independence.

A NEW GENERATION

But the times were changing. A newer generation was eager for power, and the continuing conflict with Britain was of limited interest to them. Instead, their focus was on the need for social reform, to address the differences between the "haves" and "have-nots" in Iraqi society.

They argued that the current system was not governing all the people fairly; in fact, only a handful of people were enjoying the wealth and power while the rest struggled to earn enough for daily existence. Passionate about their cause, and with the support of students and political leaders opposed to the government, this group rioted in 1952. Order was restored only when the army marched in to control its own people. For two months, the army ruled the country under martial law before the government was once more in the hands of the older leadership.

By 1953, King Faysal II was 18 years old and ready to take over the duties of ruling his kingdom. But his uncle was reluctant to completely step away from political power. So while various groups struggled to gain power politically, a similar struggle was going on within the monarchy. Hopes for a new political system under the new king grew increasingly dim as it became clear that the regent had no intention of completely handing control over to his nephew.

The development of Iraq's oil fields meant that increased riches were pouring into the country. But in the increasingly dissatisfied eyes of Iraq's younger generation, the same older leaders were enjoying all the power and wealth while making decisions at the expense of their countrymen. Many of these angry young men were in the military. They formed a group, known as the Free Officers (signifying "free" from military rules and the duty to a political authority they considered corrupt), and began to meet in secret to plan the overthrow of the government.

These young soldiers had been drafted from largely poor families, and many of them knew from personal experience the inequality of the government's distribution of resources. They had seen their own families struggle for daily food, and once they were brought into the army, they observed firsthand the fine lifestyle that politicians and some of the higher-ranking military officials were enjoying.

Abd al-Salam' Arif, 1958

Abd al-Salam' Arif addresses a crowd in the streets of An Najaf on August 9, 1958. His visit was to explain to the Shi'ite Muslim population the objectives of the revolution and the reforms it was carrying out.

While rumors swirled that violence was brewing, the Free Officers still managed a surprise attack. On July 13, 1958, army troops were ordered to march to Jordan to reinforce the Jordanian army against threats from Israel. The troops set out, but late in the evening they changed direction and marched instead to Baghdad, where they seized control of the city. Colonel Abd al-Salam'Arif led a team to the radio station, where at 5:00 A.M. on July 14 he began broadcasting messages to the public, stating that the revolution was underway and that they should rush to the streets to offer their support. At about the same time, another group of soldiers entered the royal palace. King Faysal II, his uncle, and other members of the royal family rushed out to the front courtyard, no doubt intending to surrender, but they were immediately shot and killed.

With the king and regent executed, just one more link to the old regime was left: Nuri as-Said remained a powerful and significant political figure, and continued to support Western policies and interests, even at the expense of other Arab countries. The revolutionaries felt that, in order to successfully and symbolically signal the start of a new political era, not only the royal family but also as-Said must go.

Thus, early in the morning of July 14, as soldiers were attacking the palace and assassinating the royal family, a small group of soldiers surrounded as-Said's house. Awakened by the noise (and still wearing his pajamas), as-Said slipped out the back door and escaped. The streets were crowded with people awakened by the radio broadcasts and chattering excitedly about the revolution underway. Disguised as a woman, as-Said moved quickly from the house of one friend to another as soldiers began to search the area for him. A servant in one of the houses where he was hiding spotted him, and raced for the door. Sensing that he was going to be betrayed, as-Said also raced out into the crowded streets. A young man noticed the "woman" walking nearby whose face and head was covered with a black gown but whose pajamas were peeking out underneath. He called out, "That is Nuri as-Said!" Knowing full well the fate that awaited him as soldiers turned toward him, Nuri as-Said pulled out his gun and killed himself.

The radio broadcasts that sounded throughout Baghdad on that July morning spoke of freedom, of new power for all Iraqis, of a government inspired by and working for its people. Iraq would become a republic, with a president and officials elected by the people. The men who had earlier taken Iraq into a new era, who had brought about independence, seen it through two World Wars, and shaped the fate of so many, had been erased in a hail of bullets.

Royal Possessions Scattered Across Lawn of Royal Palace, 1958

The former King Ghazi's son, King Faysal II, was assassinated by soldiers on July 14, 1958 in the courtyard of his palace in Baghdad. Also killed were the Prince Regent Abdul Illah and his wife, and other members of the royal family. In the aftermath the royal possessions were taken from the palace by mobs and scattered outside.

5

A Country
in Confusion

The men who came to power in the aftermath of the 1958 revolution had in common an overwhelming desire to bring about positive change, as well as a background in the military. Military forces had been in power once before, and then, as now, they were reluctant to hand over the government to civilian representatives.

They did take immediate steps to declare Iraq a republic whose official religion would be Islam. To emphasize ties with other Arab states, they declared that Iraq was an "integral part of the Arab nation." And rather than appointing a single person as the head of the new government, they set up a Sovereignty Council, consisting of three representatives who would be responsible for ruling the nation. But this was only a pretense: the real power and authority remained firmly in the hands of the military.

TWO MEN, TWO VIEWS

In fact, a power struggle was underway between two men who had been very involved in the revolution and who now wanted to be key players in the new government. Brigadier Abd al-Karim Qasim had led the Free Officers' movement and, as a senior military official, had quickly assumed a leading position in the new government. But Colonel Arif had headed up the march on Baghdad and had made the broadcasts announcing the revolution from the captured radio station. His voice and personality were identified by many as an important part of the launch of the new government, and he, too, sought to be a leader of the new government.

The differences between these two military leaders quickly became clear. Abd al-Karim Qasim came from an Arab family whose members included both Sunnis and Shi'ites. As a student, Qasim was remembered mainly for sitting in the back of his classes and for the fact that his family's poverty was plainly demonstrated by his shabby clothes. After an unsuccessful but brief period as a teacher, Qasim decided to join the military. It was there that he found his calling, in an environment where social class mattered less than courage and hard work. The pride in one's own country that was an important part of military training greatly impressed Qasim. It is thus not surprising that once Qasim came to power, the issues that mattered most to him included improving social conditions for the poor and emphasizing Iraq's own strength and status as an independent nation.

As head of the initial governing force, Qasim named himself head of the country's military and defense. He named Colonel Abd al-Salam' Arif his deputy commander. But Arif had a very different goal in mind for Iraq. He supported the idea of a "brotherhood of Arab nations," with all Arab countries joining together as part of a single nation, and he had assumed that his fellow military officers shared this dream. But he was wrong. A mere five days after the revolution, Arif and Qasim began to challenge each other, each taking up opposite positions on the issue of greatest importance: Would Iraq be an independent nation or would it become part of the United Arab Republic?

The two men had been friends for many years, had served together in the military, and had planned the revolution with many of the same ideals in mind. They complemented each other in style and personality— Qasim was older, more serious and quiet, while Arif was bold, outspoken, and charming. But in the ruthless world of revolutionary politics, a friend can quickly be transformed into a foe. Qasim, as the senior officer, had no intention of allowing his friend to turn Iraq away from the destiny he thought best, and he began to quietly take steps to move his friend aside.

First, he sent Arif out on tours around the country, claiming that his appearances would serve to calm down the nervous citizens and explain the revolution's plans for the future. While Arif was away, Qasim replaced pro-Arab officers with pro-Communist men who supported maintaining Iraq as an independent nation. When Arif's speeches began to receive popular attention and support, Qasim began making his own speeches, some broadcast on radio and television. By November 1958, Qasim took another step to ensure his popularity by announcing that the salaries of all government workers (which included a large percentage of the population) would be raised.

Finally, Qasim took a step to remove Arif from the country altogether and from any significant position of influence: he appointed him ambassador to the German Federal Republic. Arif decided to resign instead and remained in the country, where a steady stream of officers who favored Arab unity began to meet and plan a revolution against the new revolutionary government. A series of meetings between Qasim and Arif was never able to resolve their differences, and Arif was ultimately arrested and sentenced to death. But Qasim was unwilling to sign the paper authorizing the death of his former friend. So Arif was held in prison, with the sentence of death hanging over his head and the heads of his followers, for three long years.

POWER TO THE PARTY

Before the revolution, the few political parties that had had any significant influence were generally moderate and supported the people in power. But in order to be successful, the revolution had to persuade the Iraqi people not to accept "business as usual," with the same political leaders making decisions. As it turns out, the people were easily convinced, but problems arose when the military leaders became the established political power. The changes they were able to bring about in the lives of the Iraqi people were generally small and insignificant, and the desire for greater reform that they had sparked in the people with their revolutionary talk continued, and the people hungered for a political system that could make their lives noticeably better.

Two political parties stepped in to quietly urge the people on: the Communist Party and the Ba'th (Arab Socialist) Party. Like Qasim and Arif, these two parties split over the issue of Arab unity, with the Communists strongly favoring an independent nation of Iraq and the Ba'th party supporting the creation of a single Arab nation based on socialist principles. Not surprisingly, each party backed the leader they felt best voiced their views, and Qasim found himself supported by a Communist party whose members were frequently terroristic and favored immediate executions to eliminate opponents.

Armored Car, 1961

In Kuwait City a British armored car serves as an indicator of the Western interests that were also being threatened by neighboring Iraq's incursions into Kuwait.

Qasim did not allow this infighting to distract him from his goal of a strong Iraq. He knew that one path to greater stability lay in revenues from oil production. By 1961, he was meeting with representatives from the Iraq Petroleum Company to increase the share of Iraq's profits from oil production. The negotiations were unsuccessful, so Qasim explored another route to increasing Iraq's oil profits: he decided to claim that the tiny country of Kuwait belonged to Iraq.

Kuwait had been an independent state for only a short time before Qasim announced Iraq's claim to the land. While there was some basis to the idea of a shared ethnic and historical background between the two countries dating back to the Ottoman Empire, Iraq's claim was scarcely likely to succeed. So why did Qasim decide to announce this move to acquire Kuwaiti territory?

The answer is simple, and one that we will see repeated in the subsequent troubled history of Iraq, as well as in the political events in many nations. By announcing his claim to Kuwait, Qasim was attempting to shift attention away from battles within his own country and to rally both sides with calls that would appeal to both national pride (the Communists) and a greater Arab community (the Ba'ths).

And it also helped that Kuwait had oil—lots of it. Kuwait's agreement with the oil companies operating within its borders gave it access to an even split in all profits from the oil, making Kuwait a very rich territory.

Upon hearing of Qasim's threats and rumors of troops gathering on the border, both the Arab League and Britain (which until earlier that year had retained the territory of Kuwait) sent their own military forces in to protect the new nation. Qasim never carried out his threats of force, but he suffered the consequences. Kuwait was recognized as an independent nation by the other Arab nations, and Qasim promptly severed diplomatic relations with these countries. When the crisis ended, Qasim found himself isolated from neighboring nations and facing an even more unsettled political future.

It was only a matter of time before the forces in Iraq opposing Qasim mobilized. An earlier attempt on Qasim's life (in 1959) had been unsuccessful, and the result was even stricter government controls on all aspects of daily life in an effort to stamp out rebellion. But the Ba'th party took advantage of this government crackdown to lure supporters from the increasingly dissatisfied Iraqi citizens.

A strike by high school students proved the spark that launched another revolution. It began simply enough, with a fight between two high school students. One of the students was the son of a high-ranking military official, who quickly intervened to ensure that his son was not disciplined. On December 27, 1962, students at the high school went on strike to protest this unfair favoritism, and they were joined by students from other high schools and from the University of Baghdad. The Ba'th party quickly moved in, capitalizing on the confusion and uproar to increase the protests and unify certain parts of the military behind them. In February 1963, an attack was launched by Ba'th supporters on certain regions around Baghdad. In a gesture familiar to veterans of the earlier revolution, early fighting focused on capturing the main radio station. Once Ba'th supporters succeeded in this, broadcasts were quickly issued to the nation announcing the launch of a new government. The new president of this new government: Abd al-Salam' Arif.

The Communists did not accept this new government, and instead urged the public to rush to police stations, grab weapons, and attack the revolutionaries. Fierce fighting took place in the streets, until finally Qasim was persuaded to resign. He was taken to meet with Arif and asked Arif to let him leave the country. But Qasim would not enjoy an easy escape. A court martial was called for the very day Qasim surrendered, and he and several of his supporters were sentenced to death. During their trial, Qasim spoke proudly of all that he had accomplished, and of the important role he had played in the shaping of Iraq following the revolution. But the court was unimpressed. Qasim was led into a small room, where he was shot.

A SHORT-LIVED RULE

The first step for the new Ba'th government was to wipe clean the military ranks of those remaining officers who supported Qasim and opposed the goal of Arab unity. A series of extensive forced retirements resulted in a new group of military leaders coming to power, with Arif as their leader. Similar sweeps occurred in government offices and even schools and universities, where teachers who had favored the Communist point of view were arrested and imprisoned. While this ensured that the philosophy of the new government would be clearly voiced by all in positions of authority, it also meant that the government, military, and educational systems would be run by largely inexperienced people, some lacking any credentials other than their support of the new government.

The main focus of the new government was on three areas: reestablishing military rule (with Arif at the head as president); reinforcing the importance of Arab unity; and emphasizing the ideals of socialism, involving the nationalization of several large companies and banks. This last step was quite unpopular, and as a result Arif began to distance himself both from socialism and from the military officers who put him in power. By 1965, a new government was formed (with Arif's support) with Abd ar-Rahman Al-Bazzaz serving as premier.

Al-Bazzaz was a strong supporter of Arab unity, but he was no fan of military officials meddling in politics. Shortly after becoming premier, Al-Bazzaz called for general elections and the establishment of a representative system of government. He also took steps to support private business interests within Iraq, working to create a balance between nationalized industries and the privately held businesses that played an important role in Iraq's economy.

Arif decided to go on a speaking tour to raise public support for these new steps and to confirm his approval of Al-Bazzaz's actions. In early April 1966, Arif set out on a tour of the southern provinces. His speeches were well received, but Arif's political triumph was to be short-lived. Returning from one of these speeches the evening of April 13, Arif's helicopter crashed shortly after take-off. All aboard were killed.

Abd al-Salam' Arif Leaves Baghdad Hotel, 1963

On February 18, 1963 Abd al-Salam' Arif became the head of the new Iraqi government. Three years later he met an untimely death when his helicopter crashed shortly after take off.

The country genuinely mourned the death of Arif, and it may be due to this sentimental outpouring of grief that, in the elections that followed, Arif's older brother, Abd ar-Rahman'Arif, was elected the new president. He quickly bowed to military pressure to remove Al-Bazzaz from power, and by August 1966 the Cabinet had resigned. A subsequent series of bad decisions—poor handling of Kurdish uprisings in the north, widespread corruption among those in power, the decision not to support other Arab nations during the Arab-Israeli War of 1967—led to great unrest and dissatisfaction among the Iraqis. To make matters worse, the government never followed through on the promise Al-Bazzaz had made to call for national elections.

The government depended solely on the military to retain power. The weakness of this situation became particularly evident in 1968, when a few key military officers who had been lured away by representatives of the Ba'th Party led an attack on the president's palace.

In the predawn hours of July 17, the phone next to the president's bed rang. When he answered it, he was told by General Hardan al-Tikriti, a Ba'th officer, "You are no longer president. The Ba'th has taken control of your country. If you surrender peacefully, I can guarantee that your safety will be ensured." In attempting to determine if the call was a hoax, the president learned that the army had turned against him. Well aware of the bloody end to previous governments, he slowly walked to the palace entrance and surrendered. Only a few hours after receiving that fateful phone call, Arif was on a plane for London.

The new Ba'th regime established a new political force, the Revolutionary Command Council, and selected a new president, Ahmad Hassan Al-Bakr. Al-Bakr was responsible for the reorganization of the Ba'th Party and for ensuring the party's new success. One of his assistants was a ruthless young man who had attempted to assassinate Qasim many years earlier and who more recently had spent time in prison for trying to overthrow the government. He would join Al-Bakr in leading Iraq into a new era of Ba'th leadership. His name was Saddam Hussein.

Saddam Hussein, 1975

Saddam Hussein's ruthless style of leadership has set the tone for the modern state of Iraq.

The Politics
of Power

The modern state of Iraq is closely identified with the personality and actions of Saddam Hussein, and so it is important to study the many twists and turns that led him to the presidency. In many ways, the events that shaped Saddam Hussein as a young man would, in turn, cause him to shape the destiny of his native land.

Hussein was born on April 28, 1937, in Tikrit, a small town about 100 miles north of Baghdad. As was discussed earlier in this book, the late 1930s were a time of great political confusion in Iraq, with frequently changing governments and World War II looming on the horizon. But the town of Tikrit was far removed from the hectic swirl of political maneuvering and forces of change. Hussein's family, like the majority of people in the area, lived in a mud hut and burned cow dung for fuel. They had no electricity or running water. There was only one paved road in the entire town. Hussein's father died before he was born, and his mother, unable to take care of the infant, left him to be raised by his uncle Khairallah.

The name Saddam means "one who confronts," and Saddam's childhood, marked by sadness and violence, gave him plenty of reasons to live up to his name. His uncle, a military man, participated in the thwarted Iraqi uprising of April 1941 against British troops at the air base at Habbaniya. When the monarchy was restored and the British were back in power, those who had participated in the violence were jailed (and some even executed). Hussein's uncle was imprisoned for five years. In later years, Hussein's sympathy for his uncle's experience would become clear in his own distrust of foreign meddling in Iraqi politics and a definite disgust with the monarchy.

After his uncle was jailed, Hussein was sent back to live with his mother. By then she had remarried, and his stepfather treated him with cruelty. He was forced to steal, was subjected to frequent beatings, and lived a miserable, lonely life until his uncle was released from prison in 1947. Hussein was permitted to return to his uncle's home in Tikrit where, for the first time, at the age of 10, he was allowed to go to school. Studies were a struggle, particularly since Hussein was behind most of his fellow students, and he spent more time on practical jokes than on learning. In one particularly nasty prank, Hussein approached his teacher with open arms, gave him an apparently friendly hug, and then quickly slipped a snake under his robe.

His poor grades kept him from enrolling in the military

academy—a terrible disappointment to the young man who had dreamed of a career in the military. In fact, this dream was never forgotten. It would finally be fulfilled some 20 years later when Hussein would receive the honorary rank of general despite never having served in the military.

When Hussein was rejected by the military academy, he moved with his uncle to Baghdad in 1955 to enroll in high school. Baghdad was quite a different environment from the mud huts and dirt roads of his birthplace. The town was buzzing with political plots and tales of spies. Intrigue was everywhere and Hussein quickly was caught up in the widespread public complaints and riots that were turning Baghdad into a dangerously unstable city. The sense of dissatisfaction, the undercurrent of violence, and the plotting all were perfectly suited to Hussein's personality, and he joined the Ba'th Party at the age of 20, strongly believing in its message of Arab unity and its antigovernment activities.

When Hussein first became a member, the Ba'th Party was quite small, with only about 300 members. There were many political parties in Iraq at the time, and it is interesting that Hussein chose to join one of the less powerful ones in operation. However, the motto of the party, "One Arab Nation with an Eternal Mission," made clear its goal: the unification of all Arab peoples and countries into a single, powerful national force—a goal for which his uncle had fought many years ago against the British and for which, ultimately, he had been put in prison.

Also known as the Arab Socialist Party, the Ba'th Party swept up many young men like Hussein in its activities. The party was particularly appealing to younger Iraqi political activists because its goal of a unified Arab nation was accompanied by economic ideas that were designed to modernize Iraqi society. It was, in a way, a party that was rebelling against the ideas of an older generation of Iraqi politicians, seeking new and revolutionary ways to make life in Iraq better.

Hussein's earliest political actions involved persuading his classmates to participate in activities designed to destabilize the government. He formed a kind of political gang that roamed the streets frightening citizens and acting with violence against political opponents. At the age of 21, he was imprisoned briefly in connection with the murder of a government official, although there was ultimately not enough evidence to connect him to the crime. But the experience brought him to the attention of party officials and his next assignment was a dramatic one—to assassinate Abd al-Karim Qasim, the leader of Iraq.

FROM PARTY MAN TO WANTED MAN

While driving home from his office on the night of October 7, 1959, Qasim was attacked in his car by Hussein and several other young party members. The leader was wounded in the hail of bullets, but managed to escape. Hussein's role in the assassination attempt has been embellished in more recent years. Apparently, his actual assignment was to provide covering fire for the other attackers, who were to kill Qasim. But according to most reports, he instead opened fire himself on Qasim, no doubt confusing the rest of his fellow attackers and giving the leader's bodyguards a chance to fight back. Hussein was shot—by one of the members of his own team—and the legend of his escape includes an amazing tale of flight, first on horseback, then by swimming across the freezing Tigris River with a knife clutched between his teeth, a knife that he would use to remove the bullet from his own body when he was unable to get medical help.

Whether or not every element of this story is true, it is clear that the assassination attempt made him famous in the Ba'th Party and ensured him a warm welcome by party members living in Syria once he fled across the border. From Syria, Hussein went on to Egypt, where he became involved in political activity and, at the same time, finally graduated from high school at the age of 24.

Hussein decided to enroll in law school in Cairo but did not complete his studies. He would eventually receive a law degree, although not due to any exceptional academic effort. Nine years after dropping out of law school in Egypt, he appeared at the University of Baghdad with a pistol in his belt, surrounded by four bodyguards. The law degree was quickly produced.

During his three-year stay in Egypt, Hussein also selected his wife. His fiancée was his cousin, Sajidah Talfah, who had grown up with him in his uncle Khairallah's home. They were married when Hussein moved back to Iraq in 1963. The reason for his return: the Ba'th Party had seized power.

A PARTY IN CHAOS

On his return to Iraq, Hussein found that the Ba'th Party, and his role in it, had greatly changed. While the assassination attempt on Qasim had made Hussein some-what famous in the party at the time, three years had passed and a different group of leaders was now directing the party's activities. Rushing home with the idea that he would be involved in shaping the destiny of his country, Hussein discovered instead that he had essentially been forgotten during his absence.

The ambitious young man soon realized that political power comes not merely from daring actions, but also from networking. In the quickly shifting political environment that was Iraq at the time, it was critical to have as many friends in high places as possible, and Hussein soon set to work making himself useful to many powerful people in the Ba'th Party.

From the moment they assumed power, the Ba'ths demonstrated a preference for brute force over polite debate. They were absolutely ruthless in their treatment of political opponents, and their methods were designed not only to demonstrate their political power but also to inspire fear in anyone thinking of working against them. For example, during their first days in charge of the government, following the actual assassination of Qasim, the Ba'ths learned that rumors were circulating among the people that Qasim was not really dead, that perhaps he was in hiding somewhere and would soon return to overthrow the Ba'th regime. It did not take the new government long to decide how to put an end to that rumor. For several nights, Iraqis fortunate enough to own a television would turn it on to be greeted by the sight of Qasim's bloody body and the battered corpses of his fellow officials. The camera would even show close-ups of each of the bullet holes in Qasim's body.

The violence was not reserved just for the former government but extended also to anyone who threatened the Ba'th's power. The stately palace from which King Faysal and his family had ruled over Iraq only a short time earlier was transformed into *Qasr-al-Nihayyah*, the "Palace of the End." The place where the king had been shot to death in 1958 became the place where many political prisoners would meet even more grisly fates during the Ba'th Party's time in power. It is believed by many that one of Hussein's jobs in the new government was to serve as an interrogator, and when the Ba'th Party was finally overthrown, the horrifying evidence of torture at the palace was revealed, including electric wires with pincers, pointed iron stakes on which prisoners were forced to sit, and a machine used to chop off fingers.

While the party reacted swiftly and brutally to any political opposition, it soon became clear that the greatest threat to the Ba'ths was to be found within their own ranks. Almost as soon as it came to power, the Ba'th Party began to break apart—a victim of differing viewpoints. Some in the party felt that the changes needed to transform Iraq into the ideal Arab socialist nation should happen quickly, using force if necessary, while a different group supported working with those outside the party to achieve change more slowly. A third group tried to bridge the gap, favoring more practical approaches while at the same time pushing for socialist goals. In this group was Iraq's president, Ahmad Hassan Al'Bakr, and it was with him that Hussein was to establish an important link.

Meanwhile, the internal fighting among Ba'th members ultimately meant disaster. Unable to achieve any kind of unity, it was impossible for decisions to be made, and the party and the country descended into chaos. The more radical representatives of the party were arrested and forced out of the country, and riots quickly broke out in Baghdad. After a brief nine months in power, the Ba'ths lost control of the government, and the key party members were forced out of the country, killed, or thrown in prison.

Hussein decided to remain in Iraq, and was soon put in jail. For two years he used his prison sentence as an opportunity to network with other political prisoners and to educate himself in political strategy by reading and debating with other imprisoned members of the party. He kept in contact with Bakr by smuggling out messages in the clothes of his infant child when his wife and baby would visit him.

Young Saddam, c. 1965

The events that Hussein experienced as a boy shaped the kind of man and leader that he became. In 1965, at the age of 28, Hussein (right, in profile) was interacting with Iraqi officials and politicians and making his impact known.

Ultimately, Hussein devised an escape plan involving two of his fellow prisoners who were scheduled to appear in court with him on a certain day. As they traveled to their trial, the three prisoners pleaded with their guards to stop at a particular restaurant in Baghdad for lunch. When they agreed, Hussein and one of the other prisoners went to the bathroom and escaped out the window to a waiting getaway car.

Hussein had learned several important lessons during the Ba'th Party's first experience heading the government. He made sure that when the next opportunity came, he would be ready—and that this time he would be playing a much bigger role.

MIGHT MAKES RIGHT

Hussein's smuggled messages to Bakr did their work. As one of the few more senior Ba'th Party members still in Iraq, Bakr became a powerful force within the party as it struggled to rebuild. And Hussein was by his side, serving as assistant and right-hand man, and eventually was appointed to a key position in the party's Revolutionary Command Council, the organization responsible for directing party activities.

Hussein recognized that, in the shifting sands of Iraqi politics, one single element ensured power: physical force. The recent history of quickly changing governments proved that power was achieved not through garnering popular support or making wise political deals (although these were helpful), but rather by seizing it with force. That was why the military had so often taken over governments—they possessed in numbers and weapons the greatest force, and did not hesitate to use them. Without their own military wing, the Ba'ths had been unable to fight off the takeover of their own government. Hussein recognized that, in order to fight their way back into power, the Ba'ths would have to be willing to demonstrate, and ultimately use, sheer force.

And so they did, when then-president Arif woke up on the morning of July 17, 1968, to learn that he was no longer the leader of Iraq. Hussein was not a critical player in the early days of the "July Revolution," as it became known. Instead, he was working behind the scenes as his mentor, Bakr, joined a team of other Ba'th officials in shaping the new government. Bakr became president, but a number of other officials continued to vie for power, and the arguments and internal fighting that had doomed the Ba'th Party the first time it seized power reared their ugly heads again. But Hussein had learned his lesson well, and he quickly moved to stamp out any rivals to Bakr. One rival, the minister of defense, Ibrahim Da'ud, was sent out of the country on a mission to inspect the Iraqi troops stationed in Jordan, and then not allowed to return. The other, Premier Abd al Razzaq Nayif, was forced to leave the country by a gun-toting Hussein and his officers after he had been invited to a luncheon with President Bakr. Nayif was escorted to a waiting car and then to a plane headed for Morocco.

Within two weeks, the second phase of the "July Revolution" was completed, and power was firmly in the hands of Bakr and his choice for deputy chairman: Saddam Hussein. At the age of 31, Hussein had become the second most powerful man in Iraq.

Hussein personally chose to head up the security services of the Ba'th Party, and in this capacity, one of his first acts was to wipe out any traces of opposition. Horrifying stories exist of the brutal ways in which non-Ba'thists were removed from all government offices, including the military. Key military officers were retired and, in many cases, arrested and tortured. Their positions were all filled by men loyal only to Hussein.

For the next few years, Hussein kept a low public profile, all the time working behind the scenes to remove opponents and cement the power of the Ba'th Party. In the early days of the July Revolution, while the party was at its weakest, Hussein was at his most invisible, wisely deciding that should the government be overthrown yet again, he would be at the head of the list of those who would be removed from office. He was a loyal assistant to Bakr, and he refused to make the mistake many of his predecessors had made—seizing job titles and privileges as a right. Instead, he constantly sought ways to make the party stronger and its position at the head of the government more certain. The Ba'th Party, which had not been terribly popular at the time of the July Revolution, gradually gained members as it became clear that important government and military jobs would be granted only to party members.

By 1973, the military and security forces no longer posed a threat to the government; they were filled with Ba'th members, all loyal to the party but particularly loyal to Hussein. Political opponents had either been killed or fled Iraq. Periodically, a trial of some real or imagined group of political activists would be broadcast and the resulting executions would clearly demonstrate to the Iraqi people that an unpleasant fate awaited those who dreamed of a new system of government.

PROGRESS AND THE PRESIDENCY

Hussein used not only threats but also economic development to ensure popular support for the government. While he was still officially in the number two position in the government, it was becoming clear that more and more of the decisions were being made by Hussein. Feeling more confident of the party's success, he was more willing to step into the spotlight.

Both Hussein and the Ba'th Party benefited from the nationalization of Iraq's oil industry and the wealth that came from that oil. Some of the money was distributed to Iraqis in the form of tax cuts and pay increases; other benefits included free education from kindergarten through college. In fact, many of Hussein's programs were quite progressive, both for Iraq and for the Arab world. He led several campaigns to stamp out illiteracy, and also supported legislation guaranteeing equal pay and equal job opportunities for women (including laws passed to permit women to join the military). It was clear, however, that Hussein was moving away from an emphasis on Arab unity and focusing instead on keeping stability and power within his own country's borders.

The winds of change were blowing in the Persian Gulf, and Hussein was mindful that power, no matter how long held, could vanish in a puff of revolutionary smoke. With great concern, he saw the Shah of Iran battling for control of his nation. By 1978, the Shah (whose family had ruled Iran since the early part of the 20th century) was struggling to keep his country from descending into chaos. Riots and public demonstrations made it clear that Iraq's eastern neighbor was facing the prospect of civil war. Many felt that the riots were being encouraged by Ayatollah Khomeini, an Iranian religious leader who had been forced out of his own country and had been living in Iraq since the early 1960s. At the request of the Shah, Hussein forced the Ayatollah to leave Iraq, but the unrest in Iran was too great to be contained. The Shah was overthrown and the Ayatollah returned to rule Iran, preaching an ultraconservative message that included a plan to spread the religious fever that had sparked Iran's revolution to other nations.

Ayatollah Khomeini, 1979

In 1978 the Shah of Iran was struggling to keep his country from succumbing to a fundamentalist revolution. Ayatollah Khomeini had been driven out of Iran and into Iraq in the early 1960s, but after the Shah was overthrown he made a triumphant return to Iran on February 1, 1979.

This was not a happy message for Hussein. He decided that the rumblings on the other side of the eastern border needed a strong response, and he knew that he was the one to give it. The time had come for him to become, firmly and decisively, the undisputed leader of Iraq.

He set out on a whirlwind tour of Iraq, making speeches and visiting different locations—military bases,

Ba'th Party offices, big cities, and small towns—accompanied by the news media. Now he was ready for the spotlight, and at every opportunity he stepped into it. His speeches were printed word for word in newspapers, and his picture was everywhere. He was never outwardly disloyal to his boss, President Bakr, but the message was clear: he was the new leader in Iraq.

On July 16, 1979, nearly 11 years to the day after the Ba'th Party had taken over Iraq, President Bakr appeared on television and announced that he was ready to retire. The change in leadership did not take long. Immediately after Bakr's announcement, Saddam Hussein was sworn in as the president of Iraq.

A BLOODY BEGINNING

On July 22, six days after becoming president, Hussein called a meeting of the top 1,000 members of the Ba'th Party. Those invited no doubt expected to listen to their new leader's plans for the future, perhaps with promises for increased prestige for party members or even details of new economic goals or successes. Instead, they heard something quite different.

The meeting began with a high-level official reading a confession, in which he admitted participating in a conspiracy against the government, supposedly with the support of the nation of Syria. Hussein immediately responded, denouncing traitors and those disloyal to the party. He then announced, "The people whose names I am going to read out should repeat the slogan of the party and leave the hall." Slowly he read out a list of more than 60 names, many of them the most politically important men in Iraq. One by one they were taken from the room and executed. Others would soon follow. In the days after that meeting, many members of the Ba'th Party followed

Hussein's directions to seek out "traitors" among their former friends and colleagues. Some estimates indicate that nearly 500 men were killed during those first few days of Hussein's presidency. It is clear that he effectively eliminated any possible rivals, sparked fear among those who might have been dreaming of competing with him for power, and began a system of friend-reporting-on-friend and neighbor-spying-on-neighbor that would transform Iraq into a country in which no one was ever completely safe.

Ayatollah Khomeini, 1980

The Ayatollah's stated goal of "exporting the revolution" was a threat to all the Arab nations. Hussein stressed Iraq's role as a buffer against the spread of the Iranian revolution to its neighbors.

7

The Road
to War

At the age of 42, Saddam Hussein was a mighty force within Iraq, simultaneously serving as president, secretary-general of the Ba'th party, commander in chief, head of the government, and chairman of the Revolutionary Command Council. His presence was felt everywhere, staring down at the Iraqi people from posters, speaking decisively in newspapers and on the television and radio, even beaming up at them from the faces of gold watches. He took to popping in, unexpectedly, at hospitals and factories, showing the Iraqi people not only that he cared about them, but also that he could be anywhere and everywhere.

Hussein understood the importance of television and used it

as a way to demonstrate his connection with the Iraqi people. One of his favorite venues was a regularly televised program in which he, in disguise, would "drop in" on an ordinary Iraqi family. The family would pretend not to recognize their president. Hussein would ask them for their opinion of the government, and the family would spend several minutes praising their president and his policies. Then Hussein would take off his disguise and the family would express first their amazement and then their joy that their beloved leader was in their humble home.

But the "lighter" moments in Hussein's presidency were becoming rare as he increasingly devoted more time to dealing with pressures from his neighbor to the east. The powers in Iran were hoping to export their revolution across the border—to overthrow Hussein's government (which the strictly religious Ayatollah viewed as not nearly devout enough) and replace it with the kind of conservative, religious regime operating in Iran. This was not an idle threat. The revolution in Iran had, in part, been sparked by Shi'ite Muslims over-throwing the leadership of the Sunni regime of the Shah. In Iraq, a Sunni minority held power over the rest of the nation. Approximately 60 percent of Iraqis were Shi'ite, and they were becoming increasingly unhappy with the Ba'th party.

In June 1979, the Ayatollah's regime in Iran began broadcasting messages that urged the Iraqi population to overthrow Hussein's government. Over the next several months, at least 20 Iraqi officials were killed in bomb attacks attributed to Shi'ite activists, and in April 1980, the Iraqi deputy prime minister, Tariq Aziz, was nearly killed while giving a speech at a university in Baghdad.

The tension continued over the next several months until September 4, when Iranian forces shelled some of the towns along the Iraqi border. Hussein had had enough. On September 17, 1980, he announced that their treaty with Iran was no longer valid, and five days later, Iraq launched an attack against Iranian air bases. Iran retaliated by bombing Iraqi military and economic targets, while Iraqi armed forces crossed the border and launched additional land-based attacks.

Iraq benefited from the element of surprise in its initial attack, but Hussein's motivations were defensive rather than offensive, and this caused him to make a military mistake that would cost him and his country dearly. Rather than taking advantage of his army's initial gains and successes, he halted their advance and then tried to negotiate a cease-fire agreement. The Iraqi army, pumped up from its early success, was frustrated at seeing its efforts halted and at being denied the opportunity to press ahead and gain additional territory. While Hussein tried to work out a settlement, the Iranian forces used the time to reorganize their troops. Hussein's attempts to end the war failed, and his troops soon found themselves engaged in a life-and-death struggle with Iran's forces. Hussein's plan for a quick and decisive fight had failed. His army, and his country, would pay the price.

WAR IN THE GULF

By November 1980, Iraq's initial successes were but a memory. The Iranian army had been able to regroup and successfully maintained their position, and for the next 10 months the two armies fought fiercely over the territory, neither side gaining or losing any significant amount of land. But the number of casualties were beginning to pile up at an alarming rate.

The two countries took very different approaches to the war. In Iran, the Ayatollah urged his people to make sacrifices and to dedicate their precious resources to the war cause, since it was a holy war whose aim was pure and good. In Iraq, Saddam Hussein instead assumed a "business as usual" attitude, and initially, the Iraqi people felt only lightly the effects of the war. Food and goods were still generally available, and the only significant difference noticed in the capital was that more women were taking the jobs that previously had been held by men, more and more of whom were serving in the armed forces.

The cost of maintaining the army while shielding the Iraqi people from any kind of significant shortages was enormous. Hussein soon made it clear to his neighbors to the south and west (Kuwait and Saudi Arabia) that the war Iraq was fighting was not some minor border dispute. Indeed, the Ayatollah in Iran had made clear that his goal was to ensure the spread of Shi'ite Muslim leadership throughout the entire Gulf region. Hussein made sure that the other Gulf nations were well aware of this goal, and that Iraq's role as a buffer, shielding its neighbors from the spread of Iranian revolution, would not be able to continue without their financial support.

For many Arab nation leaders, the choice was clear. The Ayatollah's stated goal of "exporting the revolution" was a threat to all of them. They felt that the spread of Iran's Islamic revolution would mean the end of any plans for Arab unity: the aims of Arabic nationalism were generally progressive, while the Iranian movement, based on conservative religious goals, planned a very different destiny for the Gulf states. But Iraq's neighbors were hesitant about committing themselves to either side, perhaps fearing the consequences to their cities and oil fields, or perhaps not completely certain which side posed the greater threat if it should win the war. But support for the Iraqi side eventually came. First Jordan,

Iranian Soldier Battle Cry, 1982

A young Iranian soldier shouts "Allahu Akhbar," God is Great, the battle cry from the trenches during the Iran-Iraq War, in November of 1982. The Ayatollah in Iran had made clear that his goal was to ensure the spread of Shi'ite Muslim leadership throughout the entire Gulf region.

then Saudi Arabia, and finally Egypt sided with Iraq. Syria and Libya offered their support to the Iranians.

The alliances came about as the war took a new and dangerous twist. Hussein had repeatedly expressed his willingness to negotiate a settlement with the Iranians, but their response was always a scornful refusal. The Iraqi army, increasingly embattled and growing tired as they struggled to maintain their positions in Iranian territory, was becoming less and less willing to fight. Wisely sensing this change in his soldiers' morale, Hussein announced that he would pull his soldiers out of Iranian territory, claiming that they were needed to help the Lebanese fight off invading Israeli troops. The pull-out of troops began on June 20, 1982.

This action, however, did not move the Iranians toward peace. In fact, it did the opposite. A mere 23 days after the Iraqis began their retreat, Iranian troops launched a massive attack on Iraqi soil, this time targeting the important port city of Basra, which is a relatively short distance from Kuwait and Saudi Arabia. This time, Hussein had little trouble persuading the leaders of these two countries to come to his assistance. Both pledged billions of dollars in support for the Iraqi war cause, providing Hussein much-needed funds at a time when the Iraqi people were beginning to feel the effects of a war suddenly being fought inside their own borders. Aid also came from outside the Gulf, as countries such as the United States, the Soviet Union, and France provided Iraq with military supplies, intelligence reports, and food and other goods. Many of these supplies enabled Iraq to expand its production of chemical and biological weapons, which would be used, a scant 10 years later, to threaten the very allies who had come to Hussein's aid.

The war raged on for a long and devastating eight years. Hussein frequently attempted to negotiate peace, at the end asking only for an agreement that each side respect the other's government (in other words, he was asking for peace with the simple request that the Iranians agree to call off their plans to overthrow his government). Even this was ignored by the Iranians. But their unyielding posture would cost them in the end. Supplied with weapons and financial support from powerful allies, and fighting battles to defend his own soil, Hussein was able to rally the Iraqi people. The Iranian army, on the other hand, was exhausted from years of fighting on foreign land. Sensing the shift, Hussein ordered a sudden fierce attack. From February to April 1988, missiles and air attacks were launched against the largest cities in Iran. The people fled the cities in huge numbers, and the government slowly crumbled as its support vanished.

It was the beginning of the end for the Iranian initiative. Lacking enough volunteers for its army, and with the citizens who had brought them to power turning against the leaders who had led them into the war, the Iranian government began to look for a way out. The Iraqi army continued its fierce campaigns, recapturing lost ground. By July 18, 1988, Iran agreed to accept the United Nations Security Council's resolution calling for a cease-fire. It took one more month for the message to be spread along all the military bases, and then finally, the fighting was over.

THE FINAL VICTIMS

Though the war with Iran had ended, Hussein had not completed his military campaign. He had used chemical weapons sparingly during the war, only occasionally launching them against the Iranian forces and preferring to use more traditional weapons during the fiercest battles. Unfortunately, the most brutal phase of the war occurred after the cease-fire had been agreed to and the shelling on the borders had ended.

During the war, the Iranian government had taken advantage of the always unstable relationship between Iraq and its Kurdish population to incite additional fighting between them. The Kurds had been seeking their own state since the Middle East was first carved up in the aftermath of World War I—a state they had been promised but never received. Ever since, they had engaged in struggles for independence in Turkey, Iraq, and Iran. The Iranians had promised the Iraqi Kurds assistance in their efforts—and the possibility of a Kurdish region of their own—if they would fight with the Iranians against the Iraqis. Many Kurds, feeling that they had been mistreated horribly at the hands of their government, were willing to do so.

Hussein did not forget the Kurds' decision. Rather than seeking out only those who had participated in the fighting on behalf of Iran (many of whom had fled as the end of the war grew near), Hussain decided to eliminate the Kurdish "issue" altogether. Only five days after the cease-fire went into effect, Hussein launched a chemical weapon attack against 65 Kurdish villages. Iraqi warplanes and helicopters flew over their northern territory, this time bringing death to the country's own people.

Many of the Kurdish population died instantly. According to reports from villagers, the weapons were not loud. As the bombs fell, first a weak sound was heard, and then a thin, yellow mist spread out in a cloud from the area of impact. The air was filled with a foul smell, and then the villagers began to fall to the ground in a violent, choking death. One Kurdish survivor of the attack later reported: "In our village, 200 to 300 people died. All the animals and birds died. All the trees dried up. It smelled like something burned. The whole world turned yellow."

Some 100,000 refugees moved in terror toward Iraq's borders with Turkey and Iran. Those who were unable to escape were seized by Iraqi forces and divided into male and female groups. The women were sent to concentration camps; the men were executed.

When other countries learned of the brutal, murderous weapons Hussein had unleashed against his own people, the international community was outraged. Hussein was surprised by the protests from those who had been allied with him just a short while earlier. After all, he was simply eliminating his enemies. Iraq was back to business as usual.

Bombing Baghdad, 1991

When Iraq rolled its tanks across the Kuwait-Iraq border a coalition of 28 nations stood prepared to answer the Iraqi actions in Kuwait with force. Shortly after midnight on January 17, 1991 U.S. warplanes began to rain down missiles on Baghdad.

8

Storms in
the Desert

n the aftermath of the war with Iran, Saddam Hussein
found himself confronted with a crushing debt to those
countries that had aided him. Allies like the United States
and France, who had provided him with much-needed weapons
and supplies, denounced his actions against the Kurds loudly in
public, and yet in private chose to take no decisive action to back
up their harsh words. Kuwait and Saudi Arabia were demanding
repayment for loans made—a demand that angered Hussein,
since he felt that Iraq had held back the Iranian revolutionary
army, in a sense protecting its neighbors from having to fight
themselves.

When it became clear that Iraq would not be repaying its

debt in the immediate future, Kuwait decided to deal with the cash shortage in another way: it increased the amount of oil it was producing. The Organization of Petroleum Exporting Countries (OPEC), to which Iraq, Kuwait, and other oil-producing nations belonged, had certain established limits restricting how much oil each country could produce, to ensure that the price stayed at an agreed-upon cost per barrel. As Kuwait increased production, more oil became available to all buyers and the price per barrel began to drop. The loss in oil revenue was particularly damaging to Iraq, since, in the aftermath of the war, the income was desperately needed for the necessary rebuilding of war-devastated areas.

Hussein was in no mood to negotiate reasonably. He sent his foreign minister, Tariq Aziz, to a meeting of the Arab League in July 1990 to make Iraq's claims clear:

1. Kuwait and the United Arab Emirates must stop their overproduction of oil.

2. Kuwait should forgive the Iraqi debt for loans made during the war with Iran.

3. The Gulf countries should assist Iraq with its rebuilding efforts in war-torn areas.

4. Kuwait must immediately negotiate final details of border areas in dispute.

The Kuwaitis, accustomed to Hussein's frequent bluster, perhaps naively chose to ignore these demands, assuming that he was simply trying to determine a way to avoid repaying their loan. But the issue of disputed border areas should have raised red flags. The somewhat makeshift arrangements the British had made when granting Kuwait its independence in 1961 had left certain borders and territorial claims vague and in dispute.

Kuwait's fabulous oil wealth could provide Iraq with control of more than 20 percent of the world's oil production. And its location would give Iraq greater strategic access to the Gulf itself.

The next step came quickly. On August 2, 1990, an army of 100,000 Iraqi troops and 300 tanks rolled across the Kuwait-Iraq border. The Kuwaiti army, a mere 16,000 men, was no match for this invasion force. The Kuwait emir (the royal ruler of the tiny country) and his family fled their land, and the Kuwaiti armed forces quickly surrendered.

On that very day, the United Nations passed a resolution demanding Iraq's immediate withdrawal from Kuwait. Hussein refused, and four days later the U.N. passed a second resolution, this one calling for economic sanctions against the aggressor. These sanctions meant that members of the U.N. were forbidden from sending weapons, food, or supplies to Iraq, nor were they allowed to purchase Iraqi oil.

The United States was among those nations speaking out most strongly against the Iraqi invasion of Kuwait. It viewed with alarm the movement of Iraqi troops heading toward Kuwait's border with Saudi Arabia. If the Saudis were similarly overrun by Iraqi troops, Hussein would control nearly 45 percent of the world's oil and pose an economic and military threat to all the nations in the Gulf region and to all oil-importing nations. By August 9, intense negotiations between the United States and Saudi Arabia resulted in U.S. troops being deployed along the Saudi border.

During the next few tense months, several attempts at negotiations were made. To Hussein's surprise, many of his former allies joined the outcry against his seizure of Kuwait. The Iraqi people, still reeling from the effects of the war with Iran, now found themselves suffering the consequences of an economic blockade, making access to food and supplies increasingly difficult. The United Nations issued a statement declaring that force could be used against Iraq if it did not withdraw from Kuwaiti territory by January 15, 1991. And yet, Hussein refused to budge.

On January 9, 1991, the U.S. secretary of state, James Baker, met with the Iraqi foreign minister, Tariq Aziz, carrying a letter from then-U.S. president George Bush Sr. The letter, intended for Hussein, clearly warned of the consequences of ignoring the order to withdraw from Kuwaiti soil and stated that Iraq stood at the brink of war with the rest of the world. Aziz refused to carry the letter to Hussein. A coalition of 28 nations now stood prepared to answer Iraqi actions in Kuwait with force.

MISSILES TARGET BAGHDAD

Shortly after midnight on January 17, 1991, allied planes began raining missiles down on Baghdad, shelling the capital and other strategic points throughout the country. Military bases and oil fields were the most favored targets. The initial attack destroyed Hussein's presidential palace, the defense ministry, and the Ba'th Party headquarters.

The devastating attacks were called "Operation Desert Storm" by the allied forces and "the Mother of All Battles" by Saddam Hussein. Despite the pumped-up descriptions and conflicting reports of victory by each side, it was clear that the Iraqis (particularly those living in Baghdad) were suffering greatly. As shelling continued, the country's major infrastructure was crumbling, daily life was becoming increasingly difficult due to shortages of supplies, the absence of electricity or running water, and nightly rushes to air raid shelters. The oil Hussein had seized meant little if it could not be sold and if, in fact, many of the Iraqi oil fields were being simultaneously destroyed by allied bombings.

As the cost of the war weighed heavier on the Iraqi people, Hussein made a surprising announcement: He indicated that he would withdraw Iraqi troops from Kuwait, but that the withdrawal would begin when Israel began to withdraw from Palestine, the land it was currently occupying and which Hussein claimed was truly Arab territory. The attempt to link Iraqi aggression with Israel's presence in the Middle East failed.

George Bush offered another deadline: Iraqi troops must withdraw from Kuwait by February 23, 1991, or a ground war would begin. When this deadline was not met, on February 24 the allied military forces quickly penetrated Iraqi defenses and, within two days, had taken control of Kuwait and were pushing north into Iraq. Early on the morning of February 28, as the Iraqi troops either surrendered or retreated, Operation Desert Storm ended, six weeks after the fighting began. Kuwait's independence had been restored and the Iraqi army, once the fourth largest in the world, was broken.

A NEW CENTURY BEGINS

In the aftermath of the war, the Iraqi people struggled to rebuild their cities and their lives. They suffered from poverty, malnutrition, and disease. Saddam Hussein and his supporters claimed that the United Nations sanctions were responsible for the suffering of his people, but the truth was not so simple. Hussein could certainly have provided much-needed food and medicine to his people, but his focus was elsewhere—spending vast sums of money to rebuild the Iraqi military and, most experts believe, funneling additional money into the production of chemical and biological weapons.

Ultimately, the United Nations passed a resolution lifting certain portions of the trade embargo (food and money, in particular) in exchange for certain conditions to be met by Iraq, among them that Iraq take steps to destroy or remove all chemical, biological, and nuclear weapons under the supervision of United Nations inspectors. But initial attempts to inspect Hussein's weapons production facilities ended in failure. U.N. inspectors claimed that they were receiving incomplete lists of exactly where all such facilities were located, or were being denied access when they arrived at the facilities. The United States, led by then-President Bill Clinton, wanted to punish Hussein for his clear violation of the U.N. orders, but the coalition of countries that had stood up to Hussein when he overran Kuwait and threatened Saudi Arabia was less willing to back up U.N. demands this time. When Hussein ultimately ordered the U.N. inspectors to leave his country, claiming that they were merely U.S. spies, the Clinton administration was unable to rally a large group of nations to denounce Iraqi actions. Instead, as the international community witnessed the hardships the Iraqi people were suffering— hospitals without medicine, schools without supplies, families without food—it was less willing to embark on a bombing campaign that would, inevitably, visit even greater suffering upon the helpless citizens of this troubled nation.

The violence did not cease with the end of the Gulf War. Following Hussein's expulsion of the U.N. inspectors in October 1998, all U.N. staff members were evacuated from Baghdad. But, from December 16–19, 1998, U.S. and British forces launched a bombing campaign, known as "Operation Desert Fox," designed to destroy Iraq's nuclear, chemical, and biological weapons facilities. The missiles, while successfully targeting several sites, were nevertheless unable to effectively eliminate the capacity of the Iraqi government to develop these weapons of mass destruction.

The 21st century is now well under way, but Iraq still remains trapped not only by current global political and economic issues but by the legacy of the hastily drawn borders that marked off the nation in the aftermath of World War I. Many of the problems created at the beginning of the 20th century, when British politicians first attempted to determine exactly where the nation to be known as Iraq would begin and end, still spark violence among the Iraqi people today. Borders drawn on maps frequently divided tribes that had lived together for centuries, placing them in hostile countries to which they felt no loyalty. The poorly handled transition to independence left hastily patched together systems of government unable to handle the strain of competing political goals, resulting in chaotic changes in leadership and the dominance of the military. There have been periodic efforts by the Kurds in the north and the Shi'ites in the south to break away from Iraq and establish their own states. And there has been marked concern within the Arab world about the West's determination to remove Saddam Hussein from power—concern about how Iraq and the region would fare without a strong secular leader, and concern that what might come after Hussein might

Mideast Iraq Oil, 2002

On April 8, 2002 Hussein announced that he was cutting oil exports for 30 days or until Israel withdrew from the Palestinian territories.

conceivably destabilize not only that nation, but its neighbors as well.

The archeologists who combed through the ruins of ancient civilizations at the beginning of the 20th century uncovered evidence of mighty cultures marked by riches and resources. They discovered the remains of civilizations that produced the first codes of laws and the earliest forms of writing. That land that yielded up these treasures—the land we know today as Iraq—now bears only a faint resemblance to that earlier society. But it continues to play a critical role in the modern Middle East.

Gallery of Photographs
from Iraq

Gallery 1
Baghdad Scenes, c. 1910–16

Baghdad is Iraq's largest city and capital. It is located on both banks of the Tigris River near the geographic center of the country—about 330 miles inland from the Persian Gulf. Baghdad became an important city during the eighth century A.D. Through the centuries, it has survived repeated damage from wars, fire, and floods.

Census data illustrate the remarkable growth of Baghdad over the past half century—from just under 500,000 in 1947 to 1,745,000 in 1965, and from 3,226,000 in 1977 to 3,600,000 in 1987.

Along the Tigris River

Street Scene

Street Scene

Government Building with Automobile in Front

European Mason and Workers

Coffee House with Traditional Wooden Benches

House of Wealthy Merchant

Mosque and Cemetery

Quarantine Officials, Basra, 1907

These officials were photographed outside the "European quarantine house" in Basra.

At the turn of the 20th century, Ottoman officials became alarmed about the surge in communicable diseases in this major port city. Illnesses transmitted by rats harboring fleas, typhoid, and measles, and the dismal sanitary conditions led the government to force infected individuals into this quarantine house—where they were left to die isolated in squalor without medical treatment.

The two men at the right holding muzzle loaders killed those who became unruly.

Arabs Breaking Up Demonstration, Al-'Amarah, 1910

Al-'Amarah, in southeastern Iraq, was an outstanding example of autocratic rule by sheikhs who owned large estates in this rice-growing area. They maintained private armies to keep order among the tenant farmers. After the overthrow of the monarchy in 1958, most of the land around al-'Amarah was seized and redistributed as peasants swept through the area burning residences and destroying accounts and rent registers. Holdings above the maximum allowed were expropriated, with compensation paid in state bonds. But in 1969, the Iraqi government stopped payments to the former landowners. It is estimated that about 75 percent of all privately owned arable land was redistributed to the peasants.

This photograph was taken by Captain G. E. Leachman, who was honored by the Royal Geographic Society in 1911 for his surveying work in northeastern Arabia.

Fakir, c. 1910

A fakir is a Muslim or Hindu man who practices extreme self-denial as part of his religion. *Fakir* is an Arabic word meaning *poor,* especially *poor in the sight of God.* Fakirs usually live on charity and spend most of their lives in religious contemplation. They are generally regarded as holy men who are possessed of miraculous powers, such as the ability to walk on fire. Some fakirs live in religious communities while others wander about alone.

Gufa, c. 1910

Until the 1970s, gufas—huge, circular wicker boats covered with a waterproof oiled cloth—were in regular use along the Tigris and Euphrates rivers. About twenty passengers could be carried in these odd-looking crafts.

Herodotus, the fifth-century-B.C. Greek historian, described the gufa in his *History of the Greco-Persian Wars:*

The boats which came down to Babylon are circular and made of skins. The frames, which are of willow, are cut of the country of the Armenians above Assyria, and on these, which serve for hulls, a covering of skins is stretched outside, and thus the boats are made, without either stem or stern, quite round, like a shield. They are entirely filled with straw, and their cargo is then put on board, after which they float down the river. Their chief freight is wine, stored in casks made from wood of the palm tree. They are steered by two men, who stand upright in them, each with an oar, one pulling and the other pushing.

Gufas, c. 1910

The wicker construction of the gufa can be seen in this photograph, which was taken on the Tigris River near Baghdad. The serai or palace is in the background.

Kalak, 1910

The kalak, the traditional downstream transportation on both the Tigris and Euphrates rivers, was a timber raft supported on inflated goatskins that carried loads of several tons. The goatskins were inflated using a hand bellows.

    The trip from Mosul in the north to Baghdad, a distance of 225 miles, took several days. Upon arrival in Baghdad, the rafts were disassembled, the goods and timbers sold, and the the goatskins deflated and loaded on donkeys for the return trip to Mosul.

Bathing Huts, Tigris River, 1912

These bathing huts along the Tigris River were photographed by Robert I. Money, a British civil engineer who spent many years in Iraq designing numerous canals and irrigation systems.

Brushwood Dam Across the Euphrates River, 1913

Iraq is drained by the Tigris-Euphrates river system. The Tigris flows for about 880 miles and the Euphrates for some 750 miles through Iraq before they join at Qarmat 'Ali to form the Shatt al-'Arab, which flows about 120 miles into the Persian Gulf.

Establishing flood control and adequate irrigation facilities on these rivers has been a constant problem. Through the centuries, and especially in the modern era, there have been many embankments, dikes, reservoirs, canals, and man-made facilities constructed so that the rivers can be used to benefit the people.

This photograph shows a man-made brushwood dam under construction on the Euphrates River. Brushwood—small branches and thickets—are being laid across the Euphrates during its low season. Such projects require thousands of workers and an enormous amount of preparation so the dam can be completed before the river rises.

Jewish Woman, Baghdad, 1913

It is estimated that 1.5 million Jews lived for several centuries in North Africa and the Middle East. Since their ancestors never lived in Europe, they are referred to as Oriental Jews.

In the Arab lands of Morocco, Algeria, Tunisia, Libya, Egypt, Yemen, Jordan, Lebanon, Syria, and Iraq, Oriental Jews spoke Arabic as their native language.

Until 1951, non-Muslims comprised about 6 percent of the Iraqi people—and the Jews were the oldest and largest of these communities, tracing their heritage to the Babylonian captivity of the sixth century B.C. Overwhelmingly urban, most of the Jewish community lived in Baghdad.

In 1913, the population of Baghdad stood at about 180,000—135,000 Muslims, 40,000 Jews, and 5,000 others, including 40 Europeans and 1 American. Following the establishment of Israel in 1948, practically all of the Iraqi Jews migrated there.

While most of the Jews in Baghdad were poor, it is obvious from this photograph that this woman came from a prosperous family.

Kurds of Rawanduz, c. 1915

Rawanduz is a town in the hills of northeast Iraq, in an area between the Turkish and Iranian borders. The inhabitants are Kurds, an ethnic and linguistic group that numbered more than 15 million at the beginning of the 21st century.

The traditional Kurdish way of life was nomadic, revolving around sheep and goat herding throughout the Mesopotamian plains and the highlands of Turkey and Iran. However, the enforcement of national boundaries after World War I impeded the seasonal migration of their flocks, forcing most Kurds to abandon their traditional ways for village life and settled farming.

The Kurds have never known political unity. The Treaty of Sèvres (1920) abolished the Ottoman Empire and provided for an independent Armenia and an autonomous Kurdistan. However, the treaty was rejected by the new Turkish nationalist government and was replaced by the Treaty of Lausanne (1923), which omitted reference to Armenia and Kurdistan.

Kurds, 1919

Every Kurdish man, from the age of eight upward, carries a rifle and swaths himself in two or three enormous belts, or bandoleers, of cartridges.

Kurdish life probably changed very little over the centuries until the end of World War I. Then, the partition of their traditional lands by the new modern states caused the rise of Kurdish nationalism. Since 1918, the Kurds have been at war with their neighbors in attempts to gain their independence. In the 1970s, Iraq granted the Kurds limited autonomy, which they declared inadequate. Unsuccessful Kurdish rebellions have continued into the 21st century, and horrific slaughter of the Kurds has been the usual consequence.

Arab Hut in an Orange Grove, 1919

Iraq had an overwhelmingly agrarian economy until the 1950s. Most farming was conducted by sharecroppers and tenants who received only a portion—often a very small portion—of the crop.

The land tenure system under the Ottomans, and modified by subsequent Iraqi governments, provided little incentive to improve productivity. On the eve of the 1958 revolution, more than two-thirds of Iraq's cultivated land was owned by only 2 percent of the population, while, at the other extreme, 86 percent owned less than 10 percent of the land. The prerevolutionary governments were aware of these inequities in the countryside and of the poor condition of most tenant farmers. However, landlords constituted a strong political force during the monarchical era (1932–58), and they were able to frustrate remedial legislation.

The promise of land reform had kindled popular enthusiasm for the 1958 revolution. The new government began radical agrarian changes within three months of taking power.

This photograph was taken by Major Kenneth Mason, who was stationed in the Middle East during World War I. Mason was one of several British officers sent to Ottoman officials in Mosul to explain the 1918 armistice terms and the provisions for evacuation for their troops from the region. Subsequently, Mason became fascinated by the canal system of ancient Babylon. Using the writings of the Greek historian Xenophon (431 B.C.– c. 350 B.C.), Mason, with the assistance of aerial photographs, retraced the ancient canal system and verified the accuracy of Xenophon's writings.

Mudhifs Of The Marsh Arabs, c. 1950–54

The Ma'dan, a tribe of semi-nomadic marsh dwellers, live around a large swampy lake in southeastern Iraq, south of the junction of the Tigris and Euphrates rivers. The distinctive culture of these Marsh Arabs is based on the herding of water buffalo, the hunting of waterfowl, and the building of elaborate structures of woven reeds (Arabic: *mudhifs*).

All Marsh Arab houses are made from reeds. This photograph is of a "guesthouse" which, with its reed spires and vaulted door, serves as a meeting place for the town's elders. The "guesthouse" always faces Mecca. These strange-looking structures have Gothic-style arches made from bundles of reed tied together at the top. The reed walls are woven in intricate patterns. A fourth-century-B.C. plaque from the city of Uruk, on the western edge of the marsh, depicts such a structure, showing the longevity of the style.

This photograph was taken in May when the floodwaters are at their highest. The humidity in the marshes means that these giant reed constructions—some as large as 50 feet long and 15 feet wide—need rebuilding every 10 years.

Sir Wilfred Thesiger (b.1910) took this photograph, and the following two, during his 1950–54 expedition to Iraq. He used a Leica camera, which he protected from the humidity in a goatskin bag. Thesiger lived with Marsh Arabs for several years. His travels elsewhere have included the Zagros Mountains in Iran, the Hindu Kush, the Karakokram Mountains, and Nurestan in eastern Afghanistan. His autobiography, *The Life of My Choice*, was published in 1987.

138

Marsh Arab Man, c. 1950–54

Sir Wilfred Thesiger found the Marsh Arabs difficult to get to know because they are extremely suspicious of outsiders. He was the first European to live among them.

A typical village of a few hundred reed houses stands in the middle of a shallow lagoon. During the flood season, water rises inside a house and the inhabitants must squat on a raised reed platform. This platform also divides the family quarters from the area only used by the men. Floods turn the area around Marsh Arab homes into a desolate sea, where a family is often stranded like castaways. The water is always contaminated and dysentery is rife. Canoes are indispensable; without them, these people would be immobile, unable to move from one end of the village to the other.

Each reed house contains piles of quilts, cushions, and clothing. Buffalo dung for fuel dries on the house walls. The Marsh Arab staple diet consists of a bowl of rice with sour milk. Sometimes they eat wild fowl and fish caught in nets or speared, and a course of unlevened bread. Split-reed mats, sold to itinerant merchants, are the main cash product.

Wild boars terrorize these people. The tribal rifleman in the photograph is able to avoid the boar's savage charge while maneuvering the animal out of the marshes into open water, there to be shot.

The Marsh Arabs could not understand why Thesiger forsook the comforts of a town to travel among their villagers.

Marsh Arab Woman, c. 1950–54

The secluded Marsh Arab women go unveiled even in the presence of strangers. The women cook the meals, milk the buffalo, fetch the water, and knead the dough for unleavened bread, which is baked on reed trays. They eat the leftovers after the men leave the table.

A marriage among the marsh people is an occasion for great celebrating. If the bride belongs to another village, friends of the groom fetch her in their canoes— but before that, there is a feast and dancing in the bride's village without the groom present. Afterwards, the young woman is placed in the canoe with a few carpets. The procession of canoes stops at villages along the way, with the final celebration taking place in the groom's village. A man normally pays the bride's father the equivalent of three water buffalo for her.

In 1992, the Iraqi government began draining the marshlands to drive out Shi'ite guerrillas who had taken refuge there. By 1993, one-third of the area was dry—thousands of the Marsh Arabs either had moved deeper into the marshes or fled to Iran.

1920   Iraq is mandated to Britain.

1921   Faysal becomes the first king of Iraq on August 23.

1925   A constitution is adopted, specifying that Iraq will be a monarchy.

1932   Iraq is admitted to the League of Nations.

1933   Iraqi troops brutally massacre Assyrians living in the north. King Faysal dies; his son Ghazi becomes king.

1937   Saddam Hussein is born in Tikrit.

1939   King Ghazi dies in car accident; four-year-old Faysal II becomes king.

1941   British troops arrive at military base at Habbaniya; Iraqi military attempts to block additional forces. Britain attacks and establishes new government in Baghdad.

1942   Iraq declares war on Germany and officially enters World War II.

1945   Political parties are formed to strengthen the parliamentary system.

1953   King Faysal II turns 18 and begins to rule Iraq.

1958   Militia marches on Baghdad and seizes power. Royal family is killed. Iraq is declared a republic and Qasim becomes head of government.

1963   Ba'th Party overthrows government. Qasim is executed. Nine months later, Arif and military officers overthrow Ba'thist government.

1966   Arif is killed in a helicopter crash. His older brother becomes president.

1968   Ba'th Party seizes power. General Al'Bakr becomes president.

1972   Iraq nationalizes the Iraq Petroleum Company.

1979   Saddam Hussein becomes president.

1980   Iran/Iraq war begins.

1988   Cease-fire goes into effect. Hussein launches chemical weapon attack against Kurdish villages.

1990   Iraq invades Kuwait. United Nations condemns the action and later calls for economic sanctions against Iraq.

1991   U.N. forces launch attack against Iraq ("Operation Desert Storm"). War lasts for six weeks before ending when Kuwaiti independence is restored.

1996 U.N. and Iraq agree that Iraq will be allowed to export oil to buy food and medicine.

1998 Iraq refuses to cooperate with U.N. weapons inspectors. U.S. and British forces launch bombing campaign ("Operation Desert Fox") to destroy Iraq's nuclear, chemical, and biological weapons facilities.

2000 Baghdad airport reopens and Iraq resumes domestic passenger flights.

2001 U.S. and British forces launch bombing attacks near Baghdad.

BOOKS:

Bulloch, John, and Harvey Morris. *Saddam's War*. Boston: Faber & Faber, 1991.

Butler, Richard. *The Greatest Threat*. New York: Public Affairs, 2000.

Christie, Agatha. *An Autobiography*. New York: Dodd, Mead & Co., 1977.

Sifry, M.L., and C. Cerf, eds. *The Gulf War Reader*. New York: Times Books, 1991.

Simon, Reeva S. *Iraq Between the Two World Wars*. New York: Columbia University Press, 1986.

Wallach, Janet. *Desert Queen*. New York: Anchor Books, 1996.

Wellard, James. *Babylon*. New York: Saturday Review Press, 1972.

Young, Gavin. *Iraq: Land of Two Rivers*. London: Collins St. James Place, 1980.

ON THE INTERNET:

www.arab.net: news from the Middle East.

www.baghdad.com: current events in Iraq.

www.britannica.com: *Encyclopedia Britannica*'s online resource.

Associated Press. "Smithsonian Displays Relics of Iraqi Queen from 4,500 Years Ago." October 15, 1999. Posted on CNN website.

Bell, Florence, ed. *The Letters of Gertrude Bell*. Vol. 1. New York: Boni and Liveright, 1927.

Bulloch, John, and Harvey Morris. *Saddam's War*. Boston: Faber & Faber, 1991.

Christie, Agatha. *An Autobiography*. New York: Dodd, Mead & Co., 1977.

Fromkin, David. *A Peace to End All Peace*. New York: Avon Books, 1989.

Karsh, Efraim, and Inari Rautsi. *Saddam Hussein*. New York: Free Press, 1991.

Khadduri, Majid. *The Gulf War*. New York: Oxford University Press, 1988.

_____. *Republican Iraq*. New York: Oxford University Press, 1969.

_____. *Socialist Iraq*. Washington, D.C.: The Middle East Institute, 1978.

Khalidi, Walid. "Iraq vs. Kuwait: Claims and Counterclaims." In *The Gulf War Reader*. Sifry, M.L., and C. Cerf, eds. New York: Times Books, 1991.

Kramer, Samuel Noah. *The Sumerians*. Chicago: University of Chicago Press, 1963.

Miller, Judith, and Laurie Mylroie. "The Rise of Saddam Hussein." In *The Gulf War Reader*. Sifry, M.L., and C. Cerf, eds. New York: Times Books, 1991.

Morgan, Janet. *Agatha Christie: A Biography*. New York: Alfred A. Knopf, 1985.

Silverfarb, Daniel. *The Twilight of British Ascendancy in the Middle East*. New York: St. Martin's Press, 1994.

Simon, Reeva S. *Iraq Between the Two World Wars*. New York: Columbia University Press, 1986.

Waas, Murray. "What Washington Gave Saddam for Christmas." In *The Gulf War Reader*. Sifry, M.L., and C. Cerf, eds. New York: Times Books, 1991.

Wallach, Janet. *Desert Queen*. New York: Anchor Books, 1996.

Wellard, James. *Babylon*. New York: Saturday Review Press, 1972.

Young, Gavin. *Iraq: Land of Two Rivers*. London: Collins St. James Place, 1980.

INTERNET SOURCES:

www.arab.net

www.baghdad.com

www.britannica.com

www.news.bbc.co.uk

Cover: Royal Geographic Society
Frontispiece: Royal Geographic Society

page:

17: Courtesy of the CIA	82: AP/Wide World Photos
44: Hulton-Deutsch Collection/Corbis	90: Hulton/Archive by Getty Images
55: Hulton-Deutsch Collection/Corbis	95: AP/Wide World Photos
58: Hulton/Archive by Getty Images	98: AP/Wide World Photos
67: Bettmann/Corbis	103: AP/Wide World Photos
70: Bettmann/Corbis	108: AP/Wide World Photos
75: Bettmann/Corbis	116: AP/Wide World Photos
79: Bettmann/Corbis	

Unless otherwise credited all photographs in this book © Royal Geographic Society.
No reproduction of images without permission.
Royal Geographic Society
1 Kensington Gore
London SW7 2AR

Unless otherwise credited the photographs in this book are from the Royal Geographic Society Picture Library. Most are being published for the first time.

The Royal Geographic Society Picture Library provides an unrivaled source of over half a million images of the peoples and landscapes from around the globe. Photographs date from the 1840s onwards on a variety of subjects including the British Colonial Empire, deserts, exploration, indigenous peoples, landscapes, remote destinations, and travel.

Photography, beginning with the daguerreotype in 1839, is only marginally younger than the Society, which encouraged its explorers to use the new medium from its earliest days. From the remarkable mid-19th century black-and-white photographs to color transparencies of the late 20th century, the focus of the collection is not the generic stock shot but the portrayal of man's resilience, adaptability and mobility in remote parts of the world.

In organizing this project, we have incurred many debts of gratitude. Our first, though, is to the professional staff of the Picture Library for their generous assistance, especially to Joanna Wright, Picture Library Manager.

HEATHER LEHR WAGNER is an editor and writer. She has an M.A. in government from the College of William and Mary and a B.A. in political science from Duke University. She is also the author of several other volumes in the CREATION OF THE MODERN MIDDLE EAST series.

AKBAR S. AHMED holds the Ibn Khaldun Chair of Islamic Studies at the School of International Service of American University. He is actively involved in the study of global Islam and its impact on contemporary society. He is the author of many books on contemporary Islam, including *Discovering Islam: Making Sense of Muslim History and Society,* which was the basis for a six-part television program produced by the BBC called *Living Islam.* Ahmed has been visiting professor and the Stewart Fellow in the Humanities at Princeton University, as well as visiting professor at Harvard University and Cambridge University.